NEW YORK PATRIOTS

Their Lives, Contributions, and Burial Sites

JOE FARRELL • LAWRENCE KNORR • JOE FARLEY

Mechanicsburg, PA USA

Published by Sunbury Press, Inc.
Mechanicsburg, Pennsylvania

www.sunburypress.com

Copyright © 2024 by Joe Farrell, Joe Farley, and Lawrence Knorr.
Cover Copyright © 2024 by Sunbury Press, Inc.

Sunbury Press supports copyright. Copyright fuels creativity, encourages diverse voices, promotes free speech, and creates a vibrant culture. Thank you for buying an authorized edition of this book and for complying with copyright laws by not reproducing, scanning, or distributing any part of it in any form without permission. You are supporting writers and allowing Sunbury Press to continue to publish books for every reader. For information contact Sunbury Press, Inc., Subsidiary Rights Dept., PO Box 548, Boiling Springs, PA 17007 USA or legal@sunburypress.com.

For information about special discounts for bulk purchases, please contact Sunbury Press Orders Dept. at (855) 338-8359 or orders@sunburypress.com.

To request one of our authors for speaking engagements or book signings, please contact Sunbury Press Publicity Dept. at publicity@sunburypress.com.

FIRST SUNBURY PRESS EDITION: December 2024

Set in Adobe Garamond | Interior design by Crystal Devine | Cover by Lawrence Knorr | Edited by the authors.

Publisher's Cataloging-in-Publication Data
Names: Farrell, Joe, author | Farley, Joe, author | Knorr, Lawrence, author.
Title: New York patriots : their lives, contributions, and burial sites / Joe Farrell Lawrence Knorr Joe Farley.
Description: First trade paperback edition. | Mechanicsburg, PA : Sunbury Press, 2024.
Summary: The individuals from New York who played prominent roles in the founding of the USA are detailed.
Identifiers: ISBN 979-8-88819-237-5 (softcover).
Subjects: HISTORY / United States / Revolutionary Period (1775-1800) | BIOGRAPHY & AUTOBIOGRAPHY / Political.

Designed in the USA
0 1 1 2 3 5 8 13 21 34 55

For the Love of Books!

Contents

Introduction 1

George Clinton "The Father of the Empire State" 3
John Alsop Merchant House of Alsop 13
Simon Boerum "Congressman from Brooklyn" 18
James Duane Conservative Founder 21
William Duer "The Panic of 1792" 27
William Floyd Major General in the Congress 32
Horatio Gates Hero of Saratoga 37
Alexander Hamilton The Federalist 43
Elizabeth Schuyler Hamilton The General's Daughter 49
George Robert Twelves Hewes "The Shoemaker and the Tea Party" 53
John Jay The First Chief Justice 62
Rufus King The Last Feralist Candidate for President 73
Francis Lewis "All That Glitters Is Not Gold" 78
Robert Livingston The Chancellor 84
William Livingston "First Governor of New Jersey" 89
Gouverneur Morris The Penman of the Constitution 95
Lewis Morris III "The Last Lord of Morrisania" 101
Thomas Paine "The Mouthpiece of the American Revolution" 107
William Paterson Author of the New Jersey Plan 115
Philip John Schuyler Father-in-Law of Hamilton 121
Baron Friedrich Wilhelm von Steuben The Prussian General 127
Hugh Williamson "The Ben Franklin of North Carolina" 135
Henry Wisner Gunpowder Patriot 140

Sources 144
Index 148

Introduction

Following the explosion of interest in Alexander Hamilton in recent years, the first Secretary of the Treasury and victim of Aaron Burr's musket ball would be a popular choice to start a book about the Founders from New York. But, by focusing on the colony/state level, other individuals come into view. This volume details twenty-three Patriots who were leaders in the American Cause during the formation of our nation. No one contributed more on behalf of New York than George Clinton, who bridged the Colonial, Revolutionary War, and early Federal periods as a military and political leader. Clinton rose to the rank of brigadier general while also performing the role of governor and then vice president of the United States.

Yes, Alexander Hamilton makes this book, as does his wife, Elizabeth Schuyler Hamilton, and his father-in-law, Philip John Schuyler. Hamilton's life is the subject of many books, and his family circle is impressive. We but scratch the surface.

Military Generals, including Baron von Steuben, Horatio Gates, and William Floyd, are also prominent in this volume. George Robert Twelves Hewes, a common soldier who seemed to be at the center of a lot of important action, is also featured.

Important political and thought leaders also contributed from New York, including John Jay, who was an important diplomat and the first Chief Justice of the Supreme Court. Gouverneur Morris helped pen the Constitution and is interred in the Bronx. Thomas Paine, who wrote *Common Sense*, was originally buried at New Rochelle, and pieces of him might still be! Rufus King, Constitution signer and presidential candidate, is found in Jamaica, Queens. Near his homestead, now a historic landmark.

Of course, we must remember the contributions of the Livingston family, with Robert and William appearing in this volume. While William is also known as the First Governor of New Jersey, Robert was a member of the Committee of Five who drafted the Declaration of Independence, was Minister to France, and administered the oath of office to George Washington.

This is only half of our list. The remainders are important in their own right as merchants, thought leaders, or politicians. We are certain you will find some surprises and many bits not commonly known and long forgotten.

George Clinton
(1739 – 1812)

"The Father of the Empire State"

Buried at Old Dutch Churchyard
Kingston, New York

Military • Continental Congress • Governor • Vice President

George Clinton was best known as the first Governor of New York and a two-time Vice President of the United States under Jefferson and Madison. He was also an effective military leader appointed to brigadier general, favored by George Washington. Later, as an Antifederalist, he was a proponent of a Bill of Rights and was at odds with Alexander Hamilton, John Jay, and Aaron Burr in New York.

Clinton, born July 26, 1739, in Little Britain, Ulster County, New York, was one of two sons of Charles Clinton, a wealthy landowner, and his wife, Elizabeth (née Denniston) Clinton. The elder Charles was of Scots-Irish descent, born in County Longford, Ireland. Due to their Catholic heritage and unwillingness to conform to the Anglican Church, the family had been unable to recover their estates in England, so Charles organized seventy people, including relatives and friends and chartered the *George and Anne* to bring them to Philadelphia in 1729. They then established a colony in Ulster County. During the French and Indian War, Colonel Charles commanded a regiment. George's brother James also later served in the American Revolution as a general.

George Clinton

As a lad, young Clinton was tutored privately. In 1757, at age 18, he left home and became a steward's mate on the privateer *Defiance* in the Caribbean. He returned to New York in 1758 and joined the colonial forces fighting the French and Indians, enlisting in a militia unit led by his father, the colonel. They participated in the capture of Fort Frontenac, near Lake Ontario, that year, and Clinton rose to the rank of lieutenant. Clinton and his brother James were also instrumental in capturing a French vessel.

In 1759, the governor, a distant relative, appointed Clinton the Clerk of the Ulster County Court of Common Pleas, a position he held for 52 years. For the next four years, Clinton studied law with one of New York's leading legal minds, William Smith Jr., in New York City. He was admitted to the New York Bar on September 12, 1764. He then opened a law practice at Little Britain in Ulster County in 1765 and surveyed New Windsor, New York. He became district attorney for Ulster County in 1766 and was elected to the New York Colonial

Assembly in 1768, associating with the Livingston faction, which was anti-British. On February 7, 1770, Clinton married Sarah Tappen, the daughter of Peter Tappen, of Dutch ancestry. The couple had five daughters and one son: Catharine Clinton (1770–1811) married firstly to John Taylor, and secondly Pierre Van Cortlandt, Jr.; Cornelia Tappen Clinton (1774–1810) married Edmond-Charles Genêt; George Washington Clinton (1778–1813) married Anna Floyd, daughter of William Floyd; Elizabeth Clinton (1780–1825) married Matthias B. Tallmadge; Martha Washington Clinton (1783–1795); and Maria Clinton (1785–1829) married Dr. Stephen D. Beekman, a grandson of Pierre Van Cortlandt.

Clinton served in the Colonial Assembly until 1775 as an opponent of British imperialism. He motioned for the approval of the resolutions of the First Continental Congress, but this was rebuffed. Clinton warned the assembly the colonies would soon need to take up arms. Following his motions in March concerning his opposition to taxes imposed by Parliament his stature in the delegation was increased. He joined his brother James at the New York Provincial Convention in New York City on April 20, following the Battles of Lexington and Concord. A member of the New York Committee of Correspondence, Clinton, Philip Livingston, James Duane, John Alsop, John Jay, Simon Boerum, William Floyd, William Wisner, Philip Schuyler, Lewis Morris, Francis Morris, and Robert R. Livingston Jr. were elected to the Second Continental Congress on April 22.

Clinton took his seat in Philadelphia on May 15, 1775. On December 19, he was commissioned as a brigadier general in New York's militia. He was asked to defend the Highlands of the Hudson River, causing him to be absent from Congress. During this time, he saw to the building of two forts and the stretching of the chain across the Hudson.

When the Declaration of Independence was being discussed and ratified on July 4, 1776, New York did not have permission from Albany to vote in the affirmative. Though he was inclined to vote in favor, Clinton missed the opportunity to do so when he was appointed a Brigadier General in the Continental Army on July 8 with a focus on further fortifying the Hudson River region of New York. Clinton remained in the military throughout the Revolutionary War.

When New York adopted its new constitution in April 1777, Clinton ran for lieutenant governor but ended up winning the governor's

George Clinton

seat, surprising his opponents, Philip Schuyler, John Morin Scott, and John Jay. He was inaugurated as the first governor of New York State in Kingston, Ulster County, on July 30, 1777. George Washington asked Clinton to return to military duty to defend the Highlands forts, Fort Clinton and Fort Montgomery. Though they were overwhelmed by a superior force in October 1777, Clinton and 600 defenders made the British pay a high price in casualties.

As governor, Clinton was known for his poor treatment of Loyalists. He seized their estates and used the funds to pay for the government's expenses, keeping taxes down. During the winter of 1777–1778, in support of his friend, George Washington, Clinton sent food to the troops at Valley Forge. Clinton was also strongly against permitting Vermont to enter the union as a state, siding with those New Yorkers who had land claims.

In 1780, Clinton led militia raids into the Indian territories in western New York to protect settlers against Loyalists, British soldiers, and Iroquois loyal to the British. The latter had been raiding the settlements, and Clinton chased them out, raising the stature of his administration. In 1783, at Dobbs Ferry on the Hudson, Clinton and Washington negotiated with General Carleton for the evacuation of the last British troops from the United States. Clinton then became an original member of the New York Society of the Cincinnati, serving as president from 1794 to 1795. Clinton was re-elected five times as governor, serving until June 1795 and chairing the state's Constitutional Convention in 1788, though he was opposed to it largely regarding federal taxation.

As an Antifederalist, Clinton wrote letters to the newspapers in opposition to the Constitution, signing them as "Cato." Alexander Hamilton responded to these as "Caesar." Ultimately, George Clinton became more popular in New York than Hamilton and was responsible for the rapid expansion of the state and the planning for the canal system therein. Some credit Clinton for making New York "The Great Empire State." His financial management during the Confederation years made New York a net creditor to the United States, thanks to low land prices, which encouraged more sales and settlements.

Clinton's Antifederalist stance during the Constitutional debates made him the most prominent opposition candidate. He garnered less than ten percent of the vote in the 1788 election and only three electoral votes from New York. He finished seventh in the presidential election, losing to Washington and Adams. However, Clinton supported his friend, Washington, by riding to his inauguration with him in New York City. He then threw an elaborate dinner party for the new president.

In 1792, as the leading Antifederalist, Clinton again ran for president, finishing third behind George Washington and John Adams. Though Thomas Jefferson was preferred as a potential vice president, the electors could not vote for two people from the same state, Virginia, thus Clinton was the leading opposition candidate. This time, Clinton won

50 electoral votes, carrying New York and the South. Adams won the vice presidency again by finishing second with 77 electoral votes from Pennsylvania and New England. George Washington received all 132 votes possible for one candidate, winning re-election unanimously.

In 1796, though not an official candidate, Clinton finished far back in the field with only 7 electoral votes. Thomas Jefferson became the leading Antifederalist in the Democratic-Republican party with 68 votes to become John Adams' vice president. Clinton retired from politics for several years.

In 1800, after the death of his wife, Clinton was coaxed out of retirement to run for the state assembly from New York City, believing that controlling the New York State Assembly would then influence the electoral votes for New York. Clinton won and then half-heartedly threw in for the vice-presidential race, losing to Aaron Burr, who became Thomas Jefferson's vice president. However, when Burr then tried to also win the New York governor's race in 1801, Clinton ran and beat him, though he was but a figurehead for his nephew DeWitt Clinton, who ran the day-to-day activities of the office.

For the 1804 presidential election, the 12th Amendment was, in effect, defining the vice presidency as a distinct office in the electoral process. Thomas Jefferson opted to dump Aaron Burr and nominated Clinton as his running mate. He was the first person elected as Vice President via the modern process, and not as a runner-up for president. Jefferson and Clinton won in a landslide in the electoral college, 162 to 14, defeating Federalists Charles Cotesworth Pinckney and Rufus King. Clinton was sworn in as the fourth Vice President of the United States on March 4, 1805. Toasted the *Albany Register*, "George Clinton: His unwearied zeal and patriotism entitle him to the confidence of the people."

Unfortunately, Jefferson largely ignored the older Clinton, who functioned as a figurehead and struggled in his senatorial role. Jefferson hoped Clinton would be too old in 1808 to run for president at age 69, allowing for his preferred successor, James Madison, to win the office. However, Clinton was not deterred and ran for president himself in 1808. Madison, however, out-maneuvered him and offered him to be his running mate. Madison-Clinton defeated the Federalist ticket of Pinckney-King 122 to 47 in the electoral college. Clinton became the first of two men to be

George Clinton (1739–1812)

Clinton bronze statue

elected vice president for two separate presidents. John C. Calhoun was the other, serving under John Quincy Adams in 1824 and Andrew Jackson in 1828. Clinton was sworn in for his second term on March 8, 1809. Clinton opposed the foreign policies of both Jefferson and Madison, preventing the appointment of Albert Gallatin as Secretary of State. Of note, he cast the tie-breaking vote in the Senate on February 20, 1811, preventing the rechartering of the Bank of the United States.

Clinton did not make it to the end of his term, dying of a heart attack on April 20, 1812, at his home in Washington, D.C., at the age of 72. For a time, his seat in the Senate was shrouded in black. His funeral was described in the *Daily National Intelligencer*:

> The mortal remains of the late vice-president of the U. States were on Tuesday evening interred at the burial ground near the navy-yard in this city, in the presence of a concourse of people greater than ever has been gathered together in this city on any similar occasion. The shops were shot at an early hour; and a general gloom pervaded all ranks of society. The hearse with its escort reached the capitol [sic] about 4 o'clock, and the procession moved thence in about half an hour afterwards, in the order which was immortal in our last. The scene was awful and impressive. The martial parade, the glistening arms and nodding plumes of the military corps which preceded the hearse—the solemn melody of the martial band, which attuned all hearts to melancholy.

The first vice president to die in office, Clinton was initially buried in the Congressional Cemetery in Washington, D.C., but was moved to the Old Dutch Churchyard in Kingston, New York, in 1908. A monument over his grave reads, in part:

> To the memory of George Clinton . . . He was a soldier and statesman of the revolution. Eminent in council and distinguished in war, he filled with unexampled usefulness, purity, and ability, among many other offices, those of governor of his native state and vice-president of the United States. While he lived, his virtue, wisdom, and valor were the pride, ornament, and security of his country, and when he died, he left an illustrious example of a well-spent life worthy of all limitations.

Nephew DeWitt Clinton, the son of his brother James, ran unsuccessfully for president in 1812, losing to James Madison. He served as

George Clinton (1739–1812)

The grave of George Clinton.

the Governor of New York from 1817 to 1823. also served as governor of New York (1817–23); in 1812 he ran unsuccessfully for the presidency of the United States, losing to James Madison.

Bancroft Prize-winning historian Alan Shaw Taylor described Clinton as "The astutest politician in Revolutionary New York, who understood the power of symbolism and the new popularity of a plain style especially when practiced by a man with the means and accomplishments to set himself above the common people."

Many places are named after Clinton including Clinton Counties in New York and Ohio and the town of Clinton, Oneida County, New York, and Clintonville, Columbus, Ohio. Clinton's bronze statue was erected in Statuary Hall at the U.S. Capitol in 1873. He is also depicted in Trumbull's painting *Declaration of Independence* even though he did not sign the document. This same painting has been on the reverse of the two-dollar bill since 1976.

John Alsop
(1724–1794)

Merchant House of Alsop

Buried in the Trinity Church Cemetery,
New York, New York.

Continental Association

John Alsop was a successful merchant from New York City who was involved in local politics and was elected to the Continental Congress. There, he signed the Continental Association and was active in promoting boycotts against England. However, when it came time to sign the Declaration of Independence, he hesitated, citing confusion about his authority to do so. Though hopeful of reconciliation with England, Alsop continued to support the Revolutionary cause from a financial perspective. He is probably best known as the father-in-law of Rufus King and the progenitor of numerous noteworthy descendants.

John Alsop was born in 1724, in New Windsor, Orange County, New York, the eldest son of John Alsop Sr., an attorney, and his wife, Abigail (née Sackett) Alsop. The elder Alsops were both descended from sea captains, and John was also a descendant of Richard Alsop, the Lord Mayor of London, in 1597. When Alsop was a boy, his father moved the family to New York City, where he continued his law practice and became a substantial landowner.

Besides a note about "preparatory studies," Alsop's education is lost to history. He and his brother Richard learned the merchant trade and

John Alsop

established a business in New York City importing and selling dry goods and cloth. They prospered and soon became one of the great merchant houses in the city. On June 6, 1766, Alsop married Mary Frogat. On October 17, 1769, their only child, Mary Alsop, was born.

As success took root, Alsop used his leisure time for political and civic pursuits, and brother Richard retired to Middletown, Connecticut. John Alsop was elected to the New York Assembly representing New York County. He was also one of the New York Hospital Association's incorporators, serving as its first governor from 1770 to 1784.

While attending the New York Assembly, Alsop called for a meeting of delegates from all the colonies to counter the Intolerable Acts. He suggested articles be drafted and sent to King George III. The assembly could not agree which delegates should attend the newly formed Continental Congress, confused by the counties sending their own slates. In 1774, John Jay, Philip Livingston (who was Richard Alsop's business partner), James Duane, Isaac Low, and John Alsop were elected in various ways to go to Philadelphia. Alsop was elected by New York City,

John Alsop (1724–1794)

New York County, and several other counties. John Jay presented Alsop's credentials, along with the others, to vouch for them. Alsop began serving in September 1774 and was one of the signers of the Continental Association, despite its negative impact on his business. He was reelected in 1775 and served through early July 1776.

During his service in Congress, Alsop served on the Secret Committee involved in the procurement of military supplies and the assignment of Benjamin Franklin, Silas Deane, and Arthur Lee as American Commissioners in Paris. Alsop was one of the merchants involved in procuring and supplying gunpowder to the Continental Army.

While serving in the Continental Congress, Alsop continued to serve in the provincial assembly and on the Committee of Sixty, which functioned as the provisional government of New York City. These bodies were involved in boycotting British goods and funding the army.

Early in 1776, New York City became the British focus, and tensions increased among the inhabitants. In June, Alsop traveled with George Washington from Philadelphia to New York and assisted in housing and supplies for the 8000 soldiers in the army. When the British invaded in July, Alsop was faced with voting for the Declaration of Independence in Philadelphia. He refused to do so, citing the ambiguity of his authority. Many of his constituents were Loyalists or neutral, and he was unsure what his constituents wanted. He felt he did not have their consent to take such a bold step. Rather than signing the document, Alsop resigned from the Continental Congress on July 16, 1776.

In August, after the British took New York City, Alsop's home was captured by the British in Newtown, New York, on the east side of Long Island. Alsop kept working in Manhattan, but after the British took that, too, he escaped to Middletown, Connecticut, for the rest of the war.

After the war, Alsop continued his involvement with the New York Hospital and served as a vestryman at Trinity Church in Manhattan. He worked to rebuild his business in New York and was the president of New York City's Chamber of Commerce from 1784 to 1785. On March 30, 1786, his daughter Mary married Rufus King, who later signed the U.S. Constitution, was a U.S. Senator, and served as the U.S. minister to the Court of St. James, effectively the U.S. ambassador to the United Kingdom.

The grave of John Alsop.

John Alsop died at home in Newtown, New York, on November 22, 1794, at 70. He was buried at Trinity Church in Manhattan. Daughter Mary and son-in-law Rufus King were the inheritors of his vast fortune.

Nephew Richard Alsop was a member of The Hartford Wits, a group of writers associated with Yale University. He wrote the *National and Civil History of Chili*. His son, also Richard, was a partner in Alsop & Co. in Chile and Peru.

Nephew Joseph Alsop's daughter Lucy married Henry Chauncey of the New York City firm Alsop & Chauncey. He founded the Pacific Mail Steamship Company in 1848. A descendant of Joseph's married a niece of Theodore Roosevelt.

Also descended from John Alsop:
- Dr. C. Loring Brace IV, noted biological anthropologist.
- Gerald Warner Brace, writer, educator, sailor, and boat builder.

John Alsop (1724–1794)

- Charles Loring Brace, philanthropist most renowned for founding the Children's Aid Society.
- David Crosby, guitarist, singer, songwriter, and founding member of three bands: The Byrds, Crosby, Stills & Nash, and CPR.
- Floyd Crosby, award-winning American cinematographer.
- Wolcott Gibbs, editor, humorist, theater critic, playwright, and author of short stories.
- Archibald Gracie III, West Point graduate who was a Confederate brigadier general during the Civil War who died during the Siege of Petersburg.
- Archibald Gracie IV, writer, amateur historian, real estate investor, and survivor of the sinking of the RMS *Titanic*.
- Isabella Beecher Hooker, a leader in the women's suffrage movement and an author.
- Charles King, academic, politician, newspaper editor, and the ninth president of Columbia University.
- Charles King, soldier and distinguished writer.
- James G. King, businessman and Whig Party politician who represented New Jersey's 5th congressional district in the United States House of Representatives. His daughter, Frederika Gore King, married Bancroft Davis.
- John Alsop King, governor of New York from 1857 to 1859.
- Rufus King, newspaper editor, educator, U.S. diplomat, and a Union brigadier general in the Civil War.
- Rufus King, Jr., an artillery officer in the Union Army during the Civil War who received the Medal of Honor.
- Ellin Travers Mackay, 2nd wife of composer and lyricist Irving Berlin.
- Alice Duer Miller, writer and poet.
- Halsey Minor, technology entrepreneur who founded CNET in 1993.
- Mary Alsop King Waddington, author.
- Jane Wyatt, actress who played the housewife and mother on the television series *Father Knows Best* and the human mother of Spock on the science fiction television show *Star Trek*.

Simon Boerum
(1724 – 1775)

"Congressman from Brooklyn"

Buried at Green-Wood Cemetery,
Brooklyn, New York

Continental Association

Simon Boerum was a New York assemblyman and clerk in Kings County who was appointed to the First Continental Congress, where he signed the Continental Association. Boerum, a strong Patriot, did so when New York was reluctant to participate in the cause. Unfortunately, he passed away before he had an opportunity to sign the Declaration of Independence.

Boerum, born February 29, 1724, in New Lots (now Brooklyn), New York, was one of six children of William Boerum and his wife, Rachel (née Bloom) Boerum. The family was of Dutch origin, the grandfather, Jacob Willemse Van Boerum, having arrived from Holland in the 1680s and establishing holdings on the west end of Long Island. Boerum was baptized at the Flatbush Church and attended the Dutch school there.

Boerum first worked on the family farm and at their mill. In 1748, he bought a home and garden nearby and married Maria Schenk on April 30. The two lived here for the rest of their lives. Today, the site is in downtown Brooklyn near the corner of Fulton and Hoyt Streets.

Simon Boerum (1724–1775)

An early view of Brooklyn before the Revolution

In 1750, at age 26, colonial Governor George Clinton appointed Boerum a clerk in Kings County, New York, and a clerk of the New York Board of Supervisors.

Boerum and Maria had one son, John Boerum, born 1759.

In 1761, Boerum entered politics and was elected to a seat in the New York colonial Assembly.

Wife Maria died in 1771 and was interred at the Old First Reformed Church Cemetery in Brooklyn.

In 1774, widower Boerum supported the Patriot cause and was elected to the First Continental Congress in Philadelphia, representing Kings County. The colony of New York did not initially send an official delegation. That October, he joined in signing the Continental Association and the Declaration of Rights and Resolves on behalf of New York. Previously, he had opposed the Galloway Plan to attempt a reconciliation with England by creating an American parliament.

Boerum was reelected to the Continental Congress in 1775, and on April 20, 1775, served as a deputy to the Provincial Convention in New York City, attempting to contravene the British government and Loyalist assembly.

Unfortunately, Boerum fell ill and had to leave the Continental Congress in Philadelphia, returning to Brooklyn. He died suddenly on July 11, 1775, at age 51. He was initially interred with his wife at the Old First Reformed Church Cemetery in Brooklyn, but in 1848, they were exhumed and reinterred at Green-Wood Cemetery.

Boerum has been mostly forgotten in the history books, but his family name remains associated with the Brooklyn neighborhood, Boerum Hill, bordered by Schermerhorn Street on the north, Fourth Avenue on the east, either Smith or Court Streets on the west, and Warren or Wykoff Streets on the south.

A portion of the neighborhood is known as Boerum Park, located from Warren Street to Baltic Street, between Hoyt and Smith Streets.

The grave of Simon Boerum.

James Duane
(1733 – 1797)

Conservative Founder

Buried beneath the Christ Episcopal Church,
Duanesburg, New York.

**Continental Congress • Continental Association
Articles of Confederation**

This founder's biography, written by the historian Edward Alexander, was titled *A Revolutionary Conservative*. It is true that this patriot sincerely wished for the colonies to find a way to reconcile with England without having to resort to an armed rebellion. However, once that Revolution began, he became a leader of the war effort. He would serve in multiple posts during his lifetime. He represented New York in the Continental Congress, was a New York state senator, the first post-colonial mayor of New York City, and a United States district judge. His name was James Duane.

Duane was born on February 6, 1773, in New York City. His father, Anthony Duane, was an Irish Protestant from County Galway who came to the New World as an officer in the Royal Navy. He left the navy and married Eva Benson, who was the daughter of a local merchant. The couple had two sons Abraham and Cornelius. Anthony Duane grew wealthy through the purchase of land used for rental and development. His wife died, and Duane remarried Althea Ketaltas, who gave birth

James Duane

to the future founder. Ketaltas was the daughter of a wealthy Dutch merchant, and by the time their son was born, his parents were very well-to-do colonial settlers.

Duane's mother passed away in 1736, and his father died in 1747. The fourteen-year-old Duane became the ward of Robert Livingston. He received his early education at Livingston Manor. By 1754 he demonstrated a thorough command of the law, and he was admitted to the bar. From that year until 1762, he operated a private law practice in the city of his birth. He closed that practice when he became a clerk of the Chancery Court of New York.

Duane married Mary Livingston in 1759. She was the eldest living daughter of his former guardian. The couple had six children. Duane's wife influenced his political thinking. He had been a member of James Delancey's conservative political faction, which opposed British policies and at the same time opposed the use of any violence to protest these measures. Livingston did not share those views, and Duane evolved to the point of becoming a leader among New York's patriots.

In 1767 Duane became the Attorney General for the province of New York. He served as a boundary commissioner within a year, a position he would assume again in 1784. In 1774 he returned to the private practice of law. By this time, his practice was earning him 1,400 pounds a year. He owned a house in Manhattan and an estate close to Schenectady, New York, of 36,000 acres and housed more than 200 tenants. Among his clients was the Trinity Church, who he represented in legal action that resulted when heirs of Anneke Jan's claimed that they were the rightful owners of a majority of lower Manhattan, a tract of land awarded to the church by the British crown.

In 1774, Duane was among New York's representatives to the First Continental Congress meeting in Philadelphia in response to the British blockading Boston Harbor and Parliament's passage of the Intolerable Acts. The American Congress message to England was the Continental Association which Duane supported and signed. The Association took effect on December 1, 1774. It called for a trade boycott with the mother country. Congress hoped that economic sanctions would pressure the English Parliament to repeal the Intolerable Acts. Duane was one of several members of Congress who still hoped for reconciliation with England. He supported the Galloway Plan of Union, which was presented to Congress by Pennsylvania delegate Joseph Galloway. The plan called for creating an American Parliament that would act together with the Parliament of Great Britain. Congress did not accept it though its defeat was a narrow one, losing six to five on October 22, 1774.

After Duane returned to New York, he was named to the Committee of Sixty in 1775. The Committee was responsible for enforcing the boycott brought about by the Continental Association. In April of that year, he was again elected to represent his state in the Second Continental Congress. He would serve in this Congress until 1781. On May 15, 1776, Congress published a resolution saying the colonies needed to form new governments. John Adams believed this was "the most important resolution that was ever taken in America" because by forming their own governments, the colonies were in effect declaring their independence. Duane opposed the resolution and wrote to his fellow New Yorker, John Jay, that there was "no reason that our colony should be too precipitate in changing the present form of government." Despite these reservations relative to breaking with the mother country, he supported the Declaration of Independence, but due to his service with the Provincial Congress of New York, he was not present in Philadelphia to sign that document.

In July of 1776, Duane attended the New York Constitutional Convention. Apparently, by this time, he had changed his views on changing the present form of government since the purpose of the gathering was to draft a constitution to replace the colonial charter.

Duane was present in Philadelphia in 1777 when the Articles of Confederation was written. In July of 1778, he was among the signers of the document that initially united the colonies. The Articles were ratified in 1781, and Duane remained a member of the Confederation Congress until 1783.

Duane remained an active public servant after the war ended. He served as the first post-colonial Mayor of New York from 1784 until 1789. During these years, he successfully revived the city after the damage done during the war and by the British occupation. He was unsuccessful in his attempt to keep the capital of the United States in New York.

In the post-war years, Duane also served two terms in the New York State Senate. He was also one of the prominent New Yorkers who met to create the New York Manumission Society to pressure the state to abolish slavery. In 1789, President Washington nominated Duane to a seat on the United States District Court for New York City. He was confirmed by the United States Senate and served until 1794, when he retired due to health problems. On February 1, 1797, he passed away and was laid to rest beneath Christ Church in Duanesburg, New York.

As recently as 1999, there was a debate in the *New York Daily News* relative to Duane's place as a founder. The debate was prompted by

James Duane (1733–1797)

Grave of James Duane inside the chapel at Duanesburg.

then-Mayor Rudy Giuliani's decision to hang Duane's portrait in City Hall's ceremonial Blue Room. Timothy L. Collins writing in opposition to this decision, stated that Duane "was widely accused of loyalist sympathies before and during the Revolution. He was instrumental in appeasing the crown and impeding the cause of American independence." This view was answered in print by a descendant of the founder, John F. Duane, who acknowledged that while his ancestor was a "conciliator who worked to settle the differences between England and the Colonies before the Revolutionary War, he was no loyalist. Once blood was shed at Lexington on April 19, 1775, Duane became a leader in the war effort. As a member of the Committee of One Hundred, the de facto city government at the outbreak of the Revolutionary War, Duane successfully proposed that all inhabitants arm themselves." Duane's descendant went on to point out that he was instrumental in financing the Colonial Army. He was so successful that he became a trusted confidant of General George Washington. In the authors' view, John Duane presented a convincing case that James Duane be remembered as an "honorable and dedicated patriot who truly was one of the Founding Fathers of our great nation."

William Duer
(1743–1799)

"The Panic of 1792"

Buried at Grace Episcopal Churchyard,
Queens, New York.

Articles of Confederation

William Duer was a British-born financier and land speculator from New York City who was elected to the Continental Congress, where he signed the Articles of Confederation on behalf of New York. During the debates concerning the U.S. Constitution, he wrote under the pen name "Philo Publius," backing the Federalist perspective. Near the end of his life, he was caught up in the 1792 financial panic and died in debtors' prison.

Duer, born March 18, 1743, in Devon, Devonshire, England, was the son of John Duer, a wealthy plantation owner, and his wife, Frances (née Frye) Duer, the daughter of Sir Frederick Frye of Antigua. John Duer owned a villa in Devon and plantations in the Caribbean on the islands of Antigua and Dominica, which generated significant income. The couple met in Antigua and were married there.

Duer was taught by private tutors before attending the prestigious boarding school, Eton, in the northwest of London. Though underage in 1762, Duer entered the British army as an ensign, accompanying Robert Clive as his aide-de-camp as he returned to India to be the governor-general of the British East-India Company. Duer did not adjust to the climate and returned to England.

William Duer

The British government contracted Duer to build masts and rigging for the British Navy in 1764. He traveled to New York to purchase supplies and noted the potential of the American colonies. Philip Schuyler, one of the wealthiest men in New York, urged Duer to invest in the timber lands near Saratoga on the Hudson, which he did. This area became known as Fort Miller and served as Duer's first residence in New York. He set up sawmills, warehouses, and a store.

Upon his father's death in 1767, Duer inherited his father's estates in the Caribbean. He now supplied lumber from New York to the islands and the British Navy and traded extensively with Schuyler. By the early 1770s, Duer had moved to Fort Miller permanently. In 1773, he made his final trip to England to settle his affairs, sold his properties, and returned to New York.

As an English gentleman with Caribbean plantations, Duer quickly became an influential citizen in New York. He held local positions of

William Duer (1743–1799)

influence including jurist of the Charlotte County court and serving on the road commission.

In 1775, Duer was a delegate to the New York Provincial Congress and was appointed as a colonel and deputy adjutant general of the New York militia. In June 1776, he was a delegate to the New York convention to create a new state constitution. He was then elected as a state senator, serving from September 9, 1777, to June 30, 1778.

On March 29, 1777, the New York Provincial Congress elected Duer to the Continental Congress, serving until November 16, 1778. During his tenure, he was worried about the financing of the army and weary of the disagreements in Congress. However, he impressed John Adams, Robert Morris, and others with his participation on the finance committee and the "Board of War." He signed the Articles of Confederation in November 1777.

After leaving Congress, Duer returned to his business pursuits in partnership with John Holker, a French commercial agent. Robert Morris arranged contracts to supply the American army, benefitting Duer.

In 1779, Duer married Lady Catherine Alexander, a daughter of Major General William Alexander "Lord Stirling" and Sarah (née Livingston) Alexander. The wedding was at Stirling's elegant country home, "The Buildings," near Basking Ridge, New Jersey. The marriage connected Duer to the powerful Alexander and Livingston families of New York and New Jersey. The couple had eight children:

- William Alexander Duer (1780–1858) was a justice of the New York State Supreme Court and, for many years, the President of Columbia University. He married Hannah Maria Denning (1782–1862), daughter of U.S. Representative William Denning.
- John Duer (1782–1858) was a noted lawyer and jurist of New York. He married Anna Bedford Bunner (1783–1864), sister of U.S. Representative Rudolph Bunner.
- Frances Duer (1786–1869) was married to Beverley Robinson (1779–1857), grandson of merchant Beverley Robinson.
- Sarah Henrietta Duer (b. 1787) married John Witherspoon Smith, son and grandson of Princeton Presidents Samuel Stanhope Smith and John Witherspoon.

- Catherine Alexander Duer (1788–1882).
- Maria Theodora Duer (1789–1837) married Beverly Chew (1773–1851) in 1810.
- Henrietta Elizabeth Duer (1790–1839) married Morris Robinson (1784–1849), brother of Beverley Robinson and founder of the Mutual Life Insurance Company of New York.
- Alexander Duer (1793–1819) married Ann Maria Westcott (1808–1897), daughter of Colonel and New York State Senator David M. Westcott, in 1815.

Duer moved to New York City in 1783 and helped establish the Bank of New York in 1784. In 1786, he was elected to the New York Assembly. As the Constitution was signed and ratified, Duer was well connected to Robert Morris and Alexander Hamilton, Philip Schuyler's son-in-law. Duer entered into the debates about the merits of the Constitution, siding with Hamilton (who used the pen name "Publius") in three articles signed "Philo Publius" (aka Friend of Hamilton). In 1789, Hamilton became the first Secretary of the Treasury, and Duer was the first Assistant Secretary.

Duer then embarked on a scheme to speculate with government bonds involving the Bank of the United States and the Bank of New York. The goal was to buy up American debt at a discount, but the markets fluctuated wildly in early 1792, bankrupting Duer personally and resulting in the loss of significant funds to the federal government in what was known as The Panic of 1792. Secretary Hamilton, apparently not involved, requested the resignation of Duer, who refused. On March 23, 1792, Duer was arrested and thrown in debtor's prison. Historians still debate whether Duer's actions were deliberate or due to incompetence. Certainly, there was poor oversight.

While imprisoned, Duer managed to provide resources to his family via his lands in Vermont and Maine, not subject to confiscation. The end of his life was confusing, as there were contrary reports about his death. On April 17, 1799, *The Times* of Alexandria, Virginia, reported that the proceedings of the case of *United States vs. William Duer* in the District Court of the United States in Washington, D.C., was halted due to the "death of the Defendant." Other newspapers reported he was still alive. Another Alexandria paper reported Duer's death, having died in debtors' prison, on April 18, 1799. Reported the *Connecticut Gazette* of

William Duer (1743–1799)

New London, "Died, in [a] New-York prison, Col. WILLIAM DUER, aged 54, of speculating memory."

Duer was initially interred at St. Thomas Church in Floral Park, New York, in the Duer family vault. He was later exhumed and moved to Grace Episcopal Churchyard in Queens, New York.

Mrs. Duer remarried William Nelson on September 15, 1801.

Duer's noteworthy descendants include:

- Denning Duer, a grandson.
- William Duer (1805–1879), who served in the U.S. Congress representing New York, a grandson.
- James Gore King Duer, a great-grandson.
- Alice Duer Miller (1874–1942), the feminist poet and writer, a great-great-granddaughter.

The grave of William Duer.

William Floyd
(1734 – 1821)

Major General in the Congress

Buried at Westernville Cemetery,
Oneida County, New York.

**Continental Association • Declaration of Independence
Major General**

William Floyd was a wealthy farmer and merchant who was a major general in the New York state militia and a Continental Congressman who signed the Continental Association and Declaration of Independence. He was the first delegate from New York to sign the Declaration of Independence.

Floyd was born on December 17, 1734, in Brookhaven, New York, on Long Island, to Nicholl Floyd and his wife, Tabitha (née Smith) Floyd. The family was of Welsh origin, descended from Richard Floyd, who visited Jamestown, Virginia, in 1620 before settling in New York in 1640 to practice law. Circa 1688, Floyd's grandfather purchased 4400 acres from Tangier Smith's family in the Mastic Neck of the town of Brookhaven, on Long Island. Floyd's father built a house there in 1723, where Floyd was born. Floyd's siblings included sister Ruth, who married Brigadier General Nathaniel Woodhull; sister Charity, who married Continental Congressmen Ezra L'Hommedieu; and brother Charles, who married Margaret Thomas.

William Floyd (1734–1821)

William Floyd

Floyd was not formally educated despite his father's wealth. Instead, he learned etiquette and how to run the plantation. Floyd's parents died months apart in 1755, leaving the farm to young William. In 1760, he married Hannah Jones (1740–1781), the daughter of William Jones from Southampton, Long Island, New York. The couple were the parents of Nicoll Floyd (1762–1852), who married Phoebe Gelston (1770–1836), daughter of David Gelston (collector of the Port of New York); Mary Floyd (1764–1805), who married Colonel Benjamin Tallmadge, who oversaw President George Washington's spy ring; and Catherine Floyd (1767–1832), who married Reverend William Clarkson (1763–1812). Floyd became one of the wealthiest men in

New York and was often approached by Governor Johnathan Trumbull of Connecticut for loans.

Floyd was against the economic policies of the British Parliament in the 1760s and 1770s. As tensions increased with Britain, Floyd became directly involved. On August 11, 1774, he was elected a delegate to the First Continental Congress in Philadelphia. There he signed the Continental Association.

On September 5, 1775, he joined the Suffolk County Militia as a colonel. When a small British naval force gathered at Gardiner's Bay to gather supplies, Floyd's unit arrived and chased them off. He rose to the rank of major general in the militia.

Floyd was reelected to the Continental Congress, attending through July 1776, when he signed the Declaration of Independence. Later that summer, on August 17, 1776, Long Island was taken by the British and many estates were plundered. Floyd learned of this while at the Congress and wrote:

> I]s New York to be Evacuated as well as Long Island without fighting, or will our army like the Romans of old Consider the Invaluable prize for which they are Contending and with their fortitude Attack the Enemy were Ever such they can find them[?]

Floyd's family was harassed and forced to flee to Middletown, Connecticut. He left the Congress and joined them there. For seven years, the rest of the war, he was unable to return to his estate. Later in 1777, after the adoption of the new state constitution, Floyd was appointed a state senator. The following October, he again represented New York in the Continental Congress.

Hannah Floyd died in 1781 because of the strain of the estate crisis. After the war was over, in 1784, Floyd married Joanna Strong of Setauket, New York, the daughter of Benajah Strong and Martha (née Mills) Strong. The family estate on Long Island had been ransacked and all papers and records destroyed. While Floyd recovered this property, he also purchased land on the Mohawk River in upstate New York. There he built a farm, and the couple had two daughters: Ann Floyd (1785–1857),

William Floyd (1734–1821)

House of William Floyd

who married George Washington Clinton (1771–1809), son of George Clinton, the first Governor of New York and the fourth Vice President of the United States; and Elizabeth Floyd (1789–1820), who married James Platt (1788–1870), youngest son of Continental Congressmen Zephaniah Platt.

On July 4, 1787, Floyd was made a member of the Society of the Cincinnati for New York. He was elected to the First Congress in March 1789, serving until 1791. He was not reelected. He did act as a presidential elector in 1792, voting for George Washington and George Clinton.

In 1795, Floyd ran for lieutenant governor of New York with Robert Yates as a Democratic-Republican, but was defeated by John Jay and Stephen Van Rensselaer. He was again an elector for president in 1800, selecting Thomas Jefferson and Aaron Burr, and in 1804 when he selected Jefferson and George Clinton. Floyd was a member of the New York Senate for the Western District in 1808.

In 1820, Floyd was chosen as a presidential elector but did not attend the Electoral College. Martin Van Buren replaced him. At this point, he was 86, living in Westernville, New York. Floyd died on August 4, 1821, and was buried at the Westernville Cemetery in Oneida County. His widow passed in 1826. The *American Mercury* reported at the time:

Thus, another patriot of the Revolution is gone! He was one of the remaining four, viz: John Adams, Thomas Jefferson, Charles Carroll, and William Floyd, who signed the Declaration of our Independence.

The old William Floyd House at Mastic Beach on Long Island is open to visitors as part of the Fire Island National Seashore. Over 200 years, eight generations of Floyds have lived there, managing the 25-room mansion on over 600 acres. It was listed on the National Register of Historic Places in 1980. Floyd's Westernville, New York, home remains privately owned, known as the General William Floyd House. It was listed on the National Register of Historic Places in 1971.

Several public schools have been named for William Floyd, including elementary, middle, and high schools in the William Floyd School District in Brookhaven Town. There is also the General William Floyd Elementary School in Oneida County and the Floyd Memorial Library in Greenport, New York. The William Floyd Parkway in Brookhaven bears his name as does the town of Floyd in Oneida County.

Grave of William Floyd

Horatio Gates
(1727–1806)

Hero of Saratoga

Buried at Trinity Church Graveyard,
New York, New York.

Military

Horatio Lloyd Gates was a retired major in the British army who was acquainted with George Washington from as early as the ill-fated Braddock Expedition during the French and Indian War. At the outset of the American Revolution, he visited Washington at "Mount Vernon" and asked to serve in the Continental Army. Washington urged Congress to appoint him and he proved to be one of the most controversial figures in American military history.

Gates was born July 26, 1727, in Maldon, England, the son of Robert and Dorothea Gates. Due to his family's status, he obtained a military commission in 1745, serving with the 20th Foot in Germany during the War of the Austrian Succession. Following his service in Europe, he came to America at age twenty-two in the company of Edward Cornwallis, the then governor of Nova Scotia and uncle of General Charles Cornwallis. By 1754, he was promoted to captain in the 45th Foot and saw action in battles there, especially at Chignecto. He married his wife Elizabeth that year in Halifax and sold his commission to purchase a captaincy in New York.

Portrait of Horatio Gates, circa 1794,
by Gilbert Stuart.

During the French and Indian War, Gates served under General Edward Braddock in America. In early July 1755, General Braddock sent a small contingent led by Captain Gates ahead of his army that was cutting a road through the wilderness to Fort Duquesne in western Pennsylvania. Braddock was making no secret of his advance and both the occupants of the fort and the local natives were well-aware of his army. Gates secured the two Monongahela River crossings without incident. After crossing 300 yards of shallow river at the second site, Gates awaited the progress of the main column about seven hours later. They arrived marching boldly with flags unfurled and the band playing "Grenadiers' March."

Captain Beaujeu, at the fort, immediately sent his force of soldiers and native warriors into the woods around the front of Braddock's men. Using the trees for cover, the French and Indians began firing, halting the advance of the British who began returning fire in a disciplined manner. Soon, the Canadian militia and French regulars were turned back, their captain dead, but the Indians remained firing at anything in the open. Gates opened fire on the Indians with his small cannons but was thwarted by their sudden movements through the trees.

Braddock rode forward to the front of the collapsing column just when the Americans had abandoned the ranks and went to fighting Indian-style in the trees. The British stood their position in the open, firing at the natives and sometimes hitting the friendly American militia. The Indians focused their fire primarily on the officers with great result, leaving the foot soldiers with no one to give them orders. Gates received a severe bullet wound and had to give up his cannons, his men falling in with the regulars who were running out of ammunition and were scrounging for cartridges from their fallen compatriots.

Aide de camp George Washington, who had been suffering terribly from dysentery, charged into the midst, attempting to rally the men. In his report, he recorded twelve musket balls pierced his coat, but not his flesh—an example of the incredible luck he had in combat. After three hours of battle, Braddock's horse was shot out from under him. While trying to mount another, he was mortally wounded in the arm and lung. With Washington's help, Braddock was carried to the rear. The men turned and ran, some throwing their muskets to run as fast as possible. Many were shot from behind by the pursuing Indians.

When the Indians paused to scalp and plunder, Washington organized the fleeing British troops into a rear guard and then ordered the main body to bring forward medical supplies and wagons to move the wounded. The British lost 83 of 89 officers killed or wounded and nearly 900 of the 1466 men in the army. The other side lost less than 100 killed or wounded.

A few days later, as the British retreated down the road they had hacked through the wilderness, Braddock succumbed to his wounds. He was buried in the middle of the road. The wagons then rode over the grave to conceal it from the Indians. Gates made it back thanks to Washington's courage and quick action.

Elizabeth Gates gave birth to their son Robert in 1758. Meanwhile, Gates served as a major under General Monckton during the capture of

Martinique in 1762. As the war ended, Gates' opportunity for advancement disappeared. Frustrated, he sold his major's commission in England and returned to North America. In 1772, he reconnected with George Washington and settled on a modest plantation near Shepherdstown in Berkeley County, Virginia (now West Virginia).

As the Revolutionary War was commencing in May 1775, Gates went to "Mount Vernon" and offered his service to Washington. Congress then appointed Gates Brigadier General and the first Adjutant General of the Continental Army. In this role, he created the army's system of records and orders and helped to standardize the regiments from various colonies. During the siege of Boston, he was a voice of caution.

Longing for field command, in June 1776 he was promoted to Major General and given command of the Canadian Department, replacing John Sullivan, whose army was in disarray as it retreated from Quebec. By summer, his army had regrouped at Fort Ticonderoga, where he was in command of the defense of Lake Champlain. General Schuyler took over command of the Canadian Department. Gates spent the summer preparing the American fleet on the lake for defense. Benedict Arnold, an experienced seaman, was his key subordinate. Arnold then sailed to face the British in the Battle of Valcour Island in October. Though a defeat, it delayed the British advance on Ticonderoga until the following year.

With additional time bought, Gates marched some of his army south to meet up with Washington in Pennsylvania following the fall of New York City. When Washington decided to attack Trenton, Gates advised further retreat and then did so himself, leaving his men behind. Claiming illness, he headed to Baltimore to meet with the Continental Congress where he discussed his desire to take charge of the army in place of Washington. Meanwhile, Washington produced stunning victories at Trenton and Princeton, eliminating doubts about his ability.

Gates was sent back to the Northern Department but escaped blame for the fall of Ticonderoga in 1777, though he had been in command there for some time. Instead, Schuyler and St. Clair were criticized and Gates was given command of the whole department on August 4, 1777. At the Battles of Saratoga, Gates led the army to victory over General Burgoyne. However, the military action was mostly led by his subordinates including Benedict Arnold, Benjamin Lincoln, Enoch Poor, and

Horatio Gates (1727–1806)

Daniel Morgan. Arnold even took the field against Gates' orders to rally the troops in a ferocious attack. Over 5700 British troops surrendered. For this, Congress presented Gates with a gold medal. After the victory, Gates proposed invading Quebec, but Washington rejected the idea. Meanwhile, the French were now convinced to form an alliance against Great Britain in 1778.

Tensions between Washington and Gates were high as Gates tried to leverage political advantage from his victory. He insulted Washington by sending his reports directly to Congress and did not return troops to Washington that were sent to aid him. Gates' friends in Congress appointed him President of the Board of War, the civilian head of the military, making him Washington's superior despite his lower rank. Some members of Congress considered appointing Gates in place of Washington. General Conway made critical remarks about Washington in a letter to Gates. Gates' adjutant, General James Wilkinson, forwarded the letter to General William Alexander, who forwarded it to Washington. What was known as the Conway Cabal came to an end thanks to Congress ending the controversy by endorsing Washington. Gates resigned from the Board of War, apologized to Washington, and took a position in the Eastern Department in November 1778.

In May 1780, after the fall of Charleston, South Carolina and the capture of General Benjamin Lincoln's southern army, Congress voted to place Gates in charge of the Southern Department. He learned of this at home at his plantation and headed south to meet the remaining army near the Deep River in North Carolina in late July. He gathered his forces and marched south to face General Charles Cornwallis, the nephew of his mentor, at Camden, South Carolina. On August 16, his army was routed. Nearly 1000 men were captured along with the army's supplies and artillery. The most noteworthy aspect of the engagement was Gates' personal retreat on horseback of 170 miles in only three days—leaving his army behind. In October, he further learned of his son Robert's demise in combat.

Gates' reputation ruined, he returned home while Nathanael Greene took command of the Southern Department on December 3. Congress called for a board of inquiry, a step before a court-martial. He vehemently opposed such criticism. While never placed in field command

Marker honoring Horatio Gates installed by the Daughters of the American Revolution at Trinity Church Cemetery in New York City.

again, his friends in Congress repealed the inquiry in 1782. Gates then joined Washington's staff in Newburgh, New York where there were rumblings of a military coup due to the lack of fulfilled promises to the troops. Gates' subordinate, General Armstrong, was found to be organizing action against Congress. It is not clear if Gates was involved in the Newburgh Conspiracy, which was put down by Washington's appeal to the troops and to Congress.

Elizabeth Gates passed in the summer of 1783. Gates retired a widower to his estate, "Traveler's Rest" near present-day Kearneysville, Jefferson County, West Virginia. He served as vice president of the Society of the Cincinnati and president of the Virginia chapter. He attempted to marry Janet Montgomery, the widow of General Richard Montgomery, but she rebuffed him. In 1786 he married Mary Valens, a recent immigrant from England who was involved in a boarding school in Maryland. Gates sold his plantation in 1790 and freed his slaves at the urging of his friend John Adams. The aging couple then retired to an estate on Manhattan Island. Gates was elected to a single term in the New York legislature in 1800. He died on April 10, 1806, and was buried in the Trinity Church graveyard on Wall Street in New York City. His actual gravesite within the cemetery is not known but a cenotaph is placed there in his memory.

The town of Gates in Monroe County, New York is named in his honor as are several streets about New York City. In York, Pennsylvania, the General Horatio Gates House was his home during the Second Continental Congress.

Alexander Hamilton
(1755 or 1757 – 1804)

The Federalist

Buried at Trinity Churchyard,
New York, New York.

U.S. Constitution • Military • Finance • First Secretary of Tresury

When he entered this world, few, if any, would have predicted the legacy left by this Founder. During the Revolution, he served as a trusted aid on the staff of General Washington. He bravely led an attack on British defenses during the decisive Battle of Yorktown. His experience serving in the Continental Army and later in the Continental Congress convinced him that a strong national government was needed if the nation was to survive. He championed that idea during the 1787 Constitutional Convention and was a signer of the document produced by that gathering. He was the principal author of the *Federalist Papers* which proved a vital tool during the ratification process and have endured as a guide to our founding principles. He gained further distinction as the country's first Secretary of the Treasury a role in which he founded the nation's financial system. Born in the West Indies this immigrant became one of the most important and unlikeliest of our Founders. A Broadway musical has reignited interest in his life and contributions. His name, of course, is Alexander Hamilton.

There is a controversy about Hamilton's date of birth. Some historians report that he was born in 1755 while others favor 1757. There is

Alexander Hamilton portrait by John Trumbull, 1806.

evidence that supports both dates. We do know that Hamilton was born on January 11th to an out-of-wedlock mother in the West Indies. When he was a boy he wrote a vivid account of a hurricane that hit the islands. That work and the abilities he demonstrated working as a clerk impressed a wealthy group of men who offered him the chance to study in America. He enrolled at King's College in New York City.

In 1774 when he was just 19, Hamilton addressed a group of patriots who had gathered to hear a number of speakers. His anti-British sentiments impressed those gathered who shouted their support and approval when he concluded his remarks. When an artillery company was organized in the city, Hamilton was chosen as its leader. Later when Washington led his army on a hectic retreat through New Jersey, Hamilton impressed the general with both his wits and skill. Washington made Hamilton one of his top aides. He quickly became one of General

Alexander Hamilton (1755 or 1757 – 1804)

Washington's favorites and a father-son relationship developed that, from Washington's view, lasted until his death.

Hamilton distinguished himself throughout the Revolution. He showed his bravery at the decisive Battle of Yorktown when he led a successful assault on British defenses. After the victory, Hamilton ended his military career and returned to New York to study law. Before the war had ended, in 1780, Hamilton married Elizabeth Schuyler the daughter of Revolutionary War general Phillip Schuyler. The Schuylers were a powerful and wealthy New York family. Despite a later romantic transgression by Hamilton, the marriage was a happy one that produced eight children.

In 1783, Hamilton served as a representative from New York to the Continental Congress. This experience convinced him that the nation could not prosper and might not even survive under the Articles of Confederation. Hamilton wrote to New York's Governor George Clinton saying, "Every day proves more and more the insufficiency of the Confederation. The proselytes to this opinion are fading fast." Hamilton also held the belief that because any act of the Congress required the unanimous consent of the thirteen state legislatures in effect Congress had "no power."

Hamilton was among the delegates representing the state of New York when the Constitutional Convention met in Philadelphia in 1787. He shared the feelings of many of his fellow delegates when he noted that if the assembly failed to establish a stable republican government the result would be that the possibility of such a government succeeding would be "lost to mankind forever." James Madison concurred telling his fellow delegates that they "would decide forever the fate of the republican government." It is not an exaggeration to state that the very survival of the nation depended on the outcome of the convention.

Hamilton favored a strong national government which put him at odds with his fellow delegates from New York as they did not share his views. He actually left the convention on June 29th because of what he viewed as the pigheadedness of his fellow New Yorkers. He returned for a session in August and for the closing ceremony in September. Hamilton signed the Constitution though he disagreed with much of it and viewed it as an initial step to something better.

Etching of a re-imagined Hamilton and Burr duel.

Despite his reservations, Hamilton threw himself wholeheartedly in the battle to secure the ratification of the Constitution. He authored the majority of the Federalist papers which remain a primary source for divining the intent of the Founders in composing the document. George Washington was impressed by Hamilton and his fellow authors James Madison and John Jay whose work became known as *The Federalist*. Writing to Hamilton, Washington expressed his view that the papers would "merit the notice of posterity because in it are candidly and ably discussed the principles of freedom and the topics of government which will be always interesting to mankind so long as they shall be connected in civil society." The arguments defending the proposed Constitution had a direct impact on the ratification of the Constitution in key states, most notably New York.

On September 11, 1789, Hamilton became the nation's first Secretary of the Treasury. In this position, he shaped the economy of the young nation. His belief in the need for a strong federal government saw him push measures to allow the government to fund the national debt, assume the states' debts, and establish its own bank. Championing these positions often found him at odds with Washington's Secretary of State, Thomas Jefferson, and one of his co-authors of *The Federalist*, James Madison. The disagreements between Hamilton and Jefferson were instrumental in the creation of political parties in the United States.

Alexander Hamilton (1755 or 1757–1804)

Hamilton's public service career came to an end as a result of his involvement in the country's first political sex scandal. In 1791, Hamilton began an affair with Maria Lewis Reynolds. When Mr. Reynolds discovered what was going on, he began blackmailing Hamilton by threatening to inform Hamilton's wife. Reynolds was arrested for counterfeiting and hoping for some assistance, he contacted Congressman James Monroe saying he could expose a high government official who was guilty of corruption. Monroe suspected that Reynolds was referring to Hamilton. As part of a Congressional investigation, Monroe and Frederick Muhlenberg interviewed Hamilton who confessed to the affair but denied any misconduct in public office. His explanation was accepted and the parties involved pledged to keep the matter private but in 1797 a newspaper published the details of the affair. Hamilton responded by writing a detailed confession which effectively ended his public service career.

His exit from public service did not include an exit from political affairs. He was active in the 1800 campaign for president. He wrote a pamphlet critical of President John Adams who, like Hamilton, was a member of the Federalist Party. Hamilton, hoping to influence fellow Federalists, sent the document to two hundred members of his party. A Republican postmaster opened a copy and it eventually found its way into the hands of Aaron Burr who was the Republican candidate for vice president. The pamphlet was then printed in Republican papers. The result was that a number of Hamilton's Federalist supporters criticized his actions. One told him that, "some very worthy and sensible men say you have exhibited the same vanity ... which you charge as a dangerous weakness in Mr. Adams." The episode proved embarrassing for the former Secretary of the Treasury.

In 1804, Hamilton's longtime New York political rival, Vice President Aaron Burr, decided to run for the office of governor in the Empire State. Hamilton fought against Burr who was defeated in the race. Shortly after the election, the *Albany Register* published letters written by Charles Cooper who had attended a dinner party with Hamilton. Cooper noted Hamilton's opposition to Burr and reported that Hamilton had expressed "a still more despicable opinion" of the Vice President at the gathering. Burr saw this as an attack on his honor which set in motion what eventually led to the most famous duel in the history of the United States. On July 11, 1804, Hamilton was mortally wounded in that meeting. He died the following day.

Hamilton was laid to rest in New York's Trinity Churchyard Cemetery. He remains one of the country's most significant Founders. From his service during the Revolution through his championing of the Constitution and service as Secretary of the Treasury, few men played a greater role in the creation of the United States of America.

Grave of Alexander Hamilton at Trinity Church Cemetery in New York City (photo by Joe Farley).

Elizabeth Schuyler Hamilton
(1757–1854)

The General's Daughter

Buried at Trinity Churchyard Cemetery,
New York, New York.

Thought Leader

She was the second born of the eight children who survived to adulthood produced by the union of Revolutionary War general Philip Schuyler and the wealthy aristocratic Catherine van Rensselaer. For much of her youth and for a time thereafter, she lived in the shadow of her older sister Angelica who was admired for both her looks and her intellect. Both sisters would eventually catch the eye of a young man who served as one of George Washington's aides but it was the younger sister who married Alexander Hamilton becoming Elizabeth Schuyler Hamilton.

Elizabeth, who was often called Betsy, was born on August 9, 1757, in Albany, New York. While her older sister was sent to an exclusive young ladies seminary for her education Betsy received her instructions at home from her mother. As a girl, she was described as something of a tomboy who demonstrated a strong will that she would retain throughout her long and eventful life.

It was in 1780 during the Revolution that Betsy was sent to stay with an aunt in Morristown, New Jersey. It was here she crossed paths with Alexander Hamilton who, along with Washington and his troops, found themselves stationed there during the winter months. The pair

Portrait of the Elizabeth Schuyler Hamilton painted by
Ralph Earl while he was in the New York City Jail.

had actually met two years prior when Hamilton dined at the Schuyler residence. It was in Morristown that the relationship between Betsy and Hamilton blossomed. That April, with General Schuyler's blessing, they became engaged.

On December 14, 1780, Betsy and Hamilton were married at a gala ceremony staged at the Schuyler Mansion. Since their older daughter, Angelica, had eloped, the General and Mrs. Schuyler spared no expense in celebrating Betsy's wedding. As a matter of fact, General Schuyler urged the couple to take a European honeymoon but Hamilton wouldn't have it. The groom was anxious to get back to the war and he and his new wife went to New Windsor to rejoin Washington's army. It was here that Betsy began aiding Hamilton with his political writings. Portions of Hamilton's 31-page letter to Robert Morris, which illustrates his vast knowledge of finance, are written by her hand. When Betsy became pregnant with the first of their eight children, she returned to her parents' home.

Elizabeth Schuyler Hamilton (1757–1854)

Hamilton continued to press Washington for command of a unit which would see action. Washington eventually granted his request and Hamilton led a successful attack on British defenses during the decisive Battle of Yorktown. After the victory, Hamilton left the army and joined his wife in Albany before the couple settled in New York City in 1783.

In 1789, Hamilton became the nation's first Secretary of the Treasury. While he handled the finances of the country, Betsy did the same for their household. James McHenry remarked to Hamilton that Betsy had "as much merit as your treasurer as you have as Treasurer of the United States." In addition, Betsy continued to aid Hamilton in his political efforts including the work he did on *The Federalist* and his defense of the Bank of the United States.

Betsy was known for her loyalty to her husband in spite of the fact that that loyalty was not always returned. Even when he was courting her back in Morristown, he was having an affair with a local barmaid. Hamilton was attracted to women and women in kind to him and he enjoyed some success in what could be termed woman-handling throughout their marriage. The most notable failure Hamilton experienced in relation to this became known as "The Reynolds Affair."

Though Hamilton had begun his dalliances with Maria Reynolds years earlier, the affair did not become known to the public until 1797, when details appeared in a Republican paper that favored Hamilton's political rival, Thomas Jefferson. Betsy initially didn't believe the reports but Hamilton ended all speculation when he wrote and published a confession that would become known as the *Reynolds Pamphlet*. In it, Hamilton admitted to the affair and to being blackmailed by Maria's husband in order to refute charges that he had been involved in public misconduct with James Reynolds. Through it all, Betsy supported her husband.

In 1797, Betsy's sister Angelica and her husband John Church returned to the United States. The elder sister quickly assumed the leading role in New York and Philadelphia society. Hamilton and Betsy were present at many of the parties hosted by the Churches. Many noted that Hamilton spent much of his time at these soirees dancing with his beautiful sister-in-law. Once again, Betsy ignored the rumors and her legendary loyalty to both her husband and her sister never faltered.

On July 11, 1804, Hamilton was mortally wounded in his historic duel with Vice President Aaron Burr. The next day as he lay dying, he

Grave of Elizabeth Schuyler Hamilton at Trinity Church Cemetery in New York City (photo by Lawrence Knorr).

gave Betsy a letter he had written before the duel. In it, he expressed the hope of meeting her in a better world and called her "the best of wives, the best of women."

Betsy would live for fifty years as Hamilton's widow. She spent those years in the service of her husband's memory and greatness. She collected and shared his correspondence, diaries, and political writings including notes to prove that it was her husband who was the primary author of *Washington's Farewell Address*.

Betsy passed away on November 9, 1854, and was laid to rest near her husband in New York's Trinity Churchyard. When she died, she was wearing a locket that contained a yellowed piece of paper. On it was a short poem Hamilton had written for her 74 years before. The poem professed Hamilton's undying affection for the only woman he may have truly loved.

George Robert Twelves Hewes
(1742–1840)

"The Shoemaker and the Tea Party"

Buried at Grand Army of the Republic Cemetery,
Richfield Springs, New York.

Boston Massacre • Boston Tea Party • Privateer • Soldier

George Robert Twelves Hewes is not a household name, but around the time of his death, his memoirs about the American Revolution were very popular and he had become a celebrity. Hewes, who lived nearly 100 years, was a witness or participant in both the Boston Massacre and the Boston Tea Party. He was later a militiaman and privateer. More recently, historian Alfred Young wrote about Hewes in his popular history *The Shoemaker and the Tea Party*.

Hewes was born on August 25, 1742, in the South End of Boston, Massachusetts, to a poor family. He was named after his father, George, his uncle, Robert, and his maternal grandmother, whose maiden name was Twelves. When Hewes was only seven, his father, a failed tanner and soap boiler, died. His widowed mother was hard on Hewes, and at fourteen, she apprenticed him to a shoemaker named Downing, whom he disliked. Scrawny and only 5'1" tall, Hewes ran off in the spring of 1756 and attempted to join the British Army with a friend named Paul Revere but was rejected due to his size. Revere was admitted, and though turned away, Hewes' rebellious nature festered.

George Robert Twelves Hewes

According to his memoirs, after 4,000 soldiers occupied Boston in 1768, Hewes was sometimes the victim of British soldiers taking from his shop without paying, and he resented when challenged by sentries while minding his own business. He protested with other artisans who were also shirked or who had their jobs taken by moonlighting soldiers. Struggling as a shoemaker, Hewes borrowed money for a proper suit so he could court the daughter of the sexton of the First Baptist Church, Sarah "Sally" Sumner. The two married that year and eventually had fifteen children.

Hewes was present on February 22, 1770, when ten-year-old Christopher Seider was shot and killed by a customs official, Ebenezer Richardson, who later received a royal pardon. About two weeks later, on March 5, 1770, Hewes joined a mob of craftsmen in support of Edward Garrick, who was harassing Lieutenant John Goldfinch over a previous debt. The mob threw snowballs and jeered at the British soldiers who were present. In response, a soldier clubbed an apprentice wigmaker with the butt of his musket, increasing the tension. The mob dared the soldiers to fire as Richardson had done. A melee ensued, and Hewes, who was unarmed, was struck in the shoulder by Private Matthew Kilroy's musket. Other soldiers opened fire, killing five men, four of whom were friends of Hewes, including James Caldwell, whom Hewes caught as he fell dead from a wound to the chest. Returning home following what became known as the Boston Massacre, Hewes verbally confronted two British soldiers, per the official deposition he gave the next day.

Noticing Hewes's radicalism and outspokenness, the Loyalist tailor to whom he owed about $300 in modern terms sought payment of the debt. Unable to pay, and with a young bride and a baby at home, Hewes was thrown in debtors' prison in September 1770.

When Britain implemented the Tea Act, the colonists first refused to buy East India Company tea and turned ships away at the docks. After the British Navy arrived to force the unloading of the tea, Hewes was among the sixty disguised protestors at Boston Harbor on the cool moonlit night of December 16, 1773. He joined one third of the rabble, which was boarding the *Dartmouth*. Meanwhile, two other parties boarded the *Eleanor* and *Beaver*. Hewes, on account of his ability to whistle, was made "boatswain" for his party, given the responsibility to demand the keys to the tea chests from the captain. Recalled Thompson Maxwell, who was sent by John Hancock, "I went accordingly, joined the band under one Captain Hewes; we mounted the ships and made tea in a trice. In the heat of conflict, the small man with the large name had been elevated from a poor shoemaker to Captain Hewes."

Hewes described the events in his memoir:

> It was now evening, and I immediately dressed myself in the costume of an Indian, equipped with a small hatchet, which I and my associates denominated the tomahawk, with which, and a club, after having painted my face and hands with coal dust in the shop of a blacksmith, I repaired to Griffin's wharf, where the ships lay that contained the tea. When I first appeared in the street after being thus disguised, I fell in with many who were dressed, equipped, and painted as I was, and who fell in with me and marched in order to the place of our destination.

When we arrived at the wharf, there were three of our number who assumed an authority to direct our operations, to which we readily submitted. They divided us into three parties, for the purpose of boarding the three ships which contained the tea at the same time. The name of him who commanded the division to which I was assigned was Leonard Pitt. The names of the other commanders I never knew.

We were immediately ordered by the respective commanders to board all the ships at the same time, which we promptly obeyed. The commander of the division to which I belonged as soon as we were on board the ship appointed me boatswain and ordered me to go to the captain and demand of him the keys to the hatches and a dozen candles. I made the demand accordingly, and the captain promptly replied, and delivered the articles; but requested me at the same time to do no damage to the ship or rigging.

We then were ordered by our commander to open the hatches and take out all the chests of tea and throw them overboard, and we immediately proceeded to execute his orders, first cutting and splitting the chests with our tomahawks, so as thoroughly to expose them to the effects of the water.

In about three hours from the time we went on board, we had thus broken and thrown overboard every tea chest to be found in the ship, while those in the other ships were disposing of the tea in the same way, at the same time. We were surrounded by British armed ships, but no attempt was made to resist us.

We then quietly retired to our several places of residence, without having any conversation with each other, or taking any measures to discover who were our associates; nor do I recollect of our having had the knowledge of the name of a single individual concerned in that affair, except that of Leonard Pitt, the commander of my division, whom I have mentioned. There appeared to be an understanding that each individual should volunteer his services, keep his own secret, and risk the consequence for himself. No disorder took place during that transaction, and it was observed at that time that the stillest night ensued that Boston had enjoyed for many months.

During the time we were throwing the tea overboard, there were several attempts made by some of the citizens of Boston and its vicinity to carry off small quantities of it for their family use. To effect that object, they would watch their opportunity to snatch up a handful from the deck, where it became plentifully scattered, and put it into their pockets.

One Captain O'Connor, whom I well knew, came on board for that purpose, and when he supposed he was not noticed, filled his pockets, and also the lining of his coat. But I had detected him and gave information to the captain of what he was doing. We were ordered to take him into custody, and just as he was stepping from the vessel, I seized him by the skirt of his coat, and in attempting to pull him back, I tore it off; but, springing forward, by a rapid effort he made his escape. He had, however, to run a gauntlet through the crowd upon the wharf nine each one, as he passed, giving him a kick or a stroke.

Another attempt was made to save a little tea from the ruins of the cargo by a tall, aged man who wore a large, cocked hat and white wig, which was fashionable at that time. He had sleightly slipped a little into his pocket, but being detected, they seized him and, taking his hat and wig from his head, threw them, together with the tea, of which they had emptied his pockets, into the water. In consideration of his advanced age, he was permitted to escape, with now and then a slight kick.

The following morning, the harbor was awash in tea. Hewes further described:

The next morning, after we had cleared the ships of the tea, it was discovered that very considerable quantities of it were floating upon the surface of the water, and to prevent the possibility of any of its being saved for use, a number of small boats were manned by sailors and citizens, who rowed them into those parts of the harbor wherever the tea was visible, and by beating it with oars and paddles so thoroughly drenched it as to render its entire destruction inevitable.

NEW YORK PATRIOTS

The following month, the scrappy Hewes was involved in another incident that made the *Massachusetts Gazette*. He came upon Loyalist customs official John Malcolm, who was now in Boston after being tarred and feathered in Portsmouth, New Hampshire, the previous November. The zealous Malcolm, whom Hewes often harassed, was seen taking his cane to an insolent child. Hewes intervened, and the two argued. Malcolm told the lower-class Hewes to stay out of the business of gentlemen. Hewes quipped that at least he had not been tarred and feathered like Malcolm, who whirled with his cane and struck Hewes so hard on the forehead that it split open, and he was knocked unconscious. Some of the witnesses who were present carried Hewes off to be treated by Dr. Joseph Warren. Meanwhile, others who remained thought Hewes was dead. Dr. Warren was able to revive Hewes, but he bore the mark on his forehead for the rest of his life.

The following morning, Hewes went to a magistrate's office to place charges against Malcolm. Later that night, January 25, 1774, an angry mob, thinking Hewes dead, descended on Malcom's home and seized him. They dragged him onto King Street and stripped him to the waist. They covered Malcolm in tar and feathers and hauled him to the Liberty Tree, where they threatened to hang him or remove his ears if he did not apologize. Hewes showed up and attempted to stop the crowd from killing Malcolm, who complied and was released.

As Britain implemented martial law in Boston, Hewes and many other Patriots fled the city. He sent his family to his father's hometown of Wrentham and then tried to escape Boston by boat, posing as a fisherman. For nine weeks, Hewes continued a ruse that he was a fisherman, and was permitted to use his boat provided the British soldiers had first pick of the fish. When he was finally ready to escape, he applied for his fishing permit. According to his memoir, *Traits of the Tea Party, Being A Memoir of George R. T. Hewes* by Thatcher:

> Hewes was a civil man, and he made his bow to the Admiral and asked for his pass. The old gentleman, for some reason or other, looked more inquisitive than his wont.
>
> "How many are going, Hewes?" he enquired, looking him sharp in the eye.

"Three, your honor," said Hewes.

"And who will be skipper?"

"Your humble servant, Sir—for want of a better."

"Very well, Mr. Skipper Hewes!"—and here he went on to remind him of the rules and closed his discourse with warning him of all deserters, which, to be sure, had in several cases proved to be no joke, as Hewes well knew; "and now," he added, with a profound emphasis, "I know what you want—I see it in the twinkling of your eye, Skipper; but mark what I tell you—if we catch you running off—look out! Skipper—that's all—look out!"

Of course, Hewes and his comrades "ran off" after heading out into the harbor to fish. In choppy seas, they had one more guard boat to pass. The two companions hid below while Hewes addressed the captain, promising to stop there first with any fish. The captain waved him on. The companions returned atop, and no one pursued them as they landed in Lynn and headed for Newhall's Tavern, where they were taken into custody by the guards.

The following morning, Hewes and his escapees were taken before the Committee of Safety, who then sent them on to meet with General Washington, who was headquartered nearby. In the yard of the general's quarters, Washington came out and inspected them. The men removed their hats in respect, but Washington quietly told them to return them to their heads.

"I am only a man," said George, referring to his lack of nobility.

As Washington interrogated them, one of the persons present, Parson Thatcher, recognized Hewes and mentioned his uncle was a "Great liberty man." Washington then pulled Hewes aside and took him into the parlor where Hewes related his entire story to the general and answered all his questions. Satisfied and intrigued, Washington invited the rest of the men inside and treated them to lunch, with Mrs. Washington helping to serve the guests. She had just recently arrived at the camp to be with George.

After dinner, Washington offered them some money, but they declined. However, the offer for a new pair of shoes for one of the party, who had very poor shoes, was graciously accepted. Washington provided passes for the men to get through the lines and head inland to join their families. Hewes then spent the rest of the Revolution with the family in Wrentham but left for service periodically. Of his former business in Boston, he later said, "The shop which I had built in Boston, I lost; it was pulled down and burned by British troops."

In the fall of 1776, Hewes was a privateer aboard the *Diamond*, capturing three enemy vessels in the first three months. When the captain tried to extend the voyage longer without any additional prizes, Hewes joined in a threatened mutiny if the ship did not return to Providence, Rhode Island.

In 1777, Hewes served in the militia for a few months and saw action at the Battle of Rhode Island in 1778.

In 1779, Hewes was back aboard ship, sailing on the *Defence* under Captain Samuel Smedley for seven and a half months. Despite capturing four ships and thousands of dollars, the captain refused to give Hewes his share.

Hewes served on land in the militia in 1780 and 1781. The following year, he hired a substitute to avoid the draft, the pressures of family weighed too heavily.

The Hewes family continued to live in Wrentham through the beginning of the War of 1812. It is believed eleven of the fifteen Hewes children survived. Two of his sons volunteered for the militia in 1812.

After the war, Hewes and his wife moved to Richland Springs in Otsego County, New York, close to some of their children. Hewes continued his shoemaking business, even in old age. As the fiftieth anniversary of the Revolution occurred in 1826, organizers began looking for the few remaining veterans in the community. Hewes was one.

Wife Sarah Hewes died in 1828 at age 77. Hewes, now a widower, continued to be recognized for his long-ago service in the Revolution. Soon, he was the oldest surviving member of the community who had direct involvement. He would appear at festivities in his militia uniform every July 4th.

One day, in the 1830s, writer James Hawkes "discovered" Hewes and wrote a biography titled *A Retrospect of the Boston Tea-Party*. The book sold very well, and Hewes toured New England in 1835, achieving celebrity status. He was a guest of honor at a celebration with the

George Robert Twelves Hewes (1742–1840)

last surviving members of the Tea Party. He sat for a portrait by Joseph Cole called *The Centenarian* which still hangs in the Old State House in Boston. A second biography, *Traits of the Tea Party* by attorney Benjamin Bussey Thatcher, followed.

Unfortunately, on July 4, 1840, while boarding a carriage to attend the annual festivities, Hewes was injured in an accident. He died November 5, 1840, at 98, though some believed him to be 109. He was buried without any commemoration at Richland Springs. In 1896, Hewes was reburied with a proper ceremony at the Grand Army of the Republic Cemetery among other veterans.

Historians have been amazed at how connected Hewes appeared to have been, interacting with some of the most famous people of his age. Many have challenged his veracity, but the stories and records available have been checked out, and no one has been able to disprove his eyewitness accounts.

Historian and biographer Alfred Young summed up Hewes: "He was a nobody who briefly became a somebody in the Revolution and, for a moment near the end of his life, a hero."

Grave of George Robert Twelves Hewes

John Jay
(1745 – 1829)

The First Chief Justice

Buried at John Jay Cemetery,
Rye, New York.

**Continental Association • President of Congress
Secretary of Foreign Affairs • United States Supreme Court**

This accomplished founder served the young country in multiple positions during his long public career. He was elected to the first and second Continental Congress where, in the latter, he also presided as the President of Congress. During the Revolutionary War, he represented the United States in Spain. He followed that by joining the American team assigned to negotiate the Treaty of Paris with England, which ended the war. Under the Articles of Confederation, he ably filled the position of Secretary of Foreign Affairs. A vocal proponent of a strong national government, he was a co-author of the *Federalist Papers*, which set forth the arguments in favor of the ratification of the United States Constitution. President Washington chose him to be the first Chief Justice of the Supreme Court. While serving in that post, he negotiated the controversial Jay Treaty with Great Britain. He concluded his career as a two-term Governor of New York. His name was John Jay.

Jay was born on December 12, 1745, in New York City. His father, Peter Jay, was a wealthy merchant who traded in furs, timber, and other

John Jay (1745–1829)

John Jay

products. His mother was Mary Van Cortlandt, who could trace Dutch ancestry and whose father served in the New York Assembly and was twice elected mayor of New York during colonial times. The Jays had ten children, seven of which survived to adulthood. Three months after their son John was born, the Jays left New York City and settled in Rye, New York.

Jay was educated at home by his mother until he was eight years of age, when he was sent to continue his schooling under the guidance of an Anglican priest. In 1760, at the age of 14, he entered King's College (now Columbia). Among the friends he made at Columbia was Robert Livingston, a man who would later become one of Jay's staunch critics. After graduating, he studied the law and was admitted to the New York bar in 1768. He and Robert Livingston then agreed to work together as partners. At the time, partnerships among attorneys were rare, but Jay and Livingston believed by working together and utilizing their connections, they were likely to attract more clients. The partnership lasted two years, after which the pair, both feeling they were on a successful path, opened law practices of their own.

During this period, Jay found time for other pursuits besides handling his legal work. According to one of his biographers, Walter Stahr, in his work *John Jay Founding Father*, the young lawyer was a leading member of a group known as the "Social Club" and was the manager of a dancing assembly. Stahr surmises that it was at a dance where Jay met Sarah Livingston in 1772 or 1773. Livingston, the eldest daughter of New Jersey Governor William Livingston, was sixteen years at the time but known for her intelligence and beauty. One of Jay's friends and fellow founder, Gouverneur Morris wrote of her, "never was a creature so admired." Jay married Livingston in the parlor of her father's home on April 28, 1774. The couple would have six children, and Sarah Livingston would be a major support and influence on Jay throughout her life. In his work on Jay, Stahr describes Sarah as "an ardent American patriot, perhaps more vocal than her restrained husband."

As the newlyweds spent their honeymoon in New York's northern counties, there was political activity in New York City. In response to the punitive measures imposed on Boston as a result of the Boston Tea Party, New Yorkers had appointed a committee to "take into consideration the measures of Parliament relative to Boston." When Jay and his wife returned to the city in late May, Jay learned that he had been named to this committee. At the initial meeting of this group consisting of 51 men, Jay was appointed to a subcommittee of four assigned to prepare a response to a letter the New Yorkers had received from Boston. The subcommittee drafted a letter that called for a meeting of delegates from all the colonies to review the situation in Boston and determine how to protect "our common rights." In July, the committee of 51 appointed Jay and four others to represent New York at the Continental Congress.

On September 5, 1774, the delegates to the First Continental Congress met in Philadelphia. The early meetings generally took care of housekeeping items, such as choosing Charles Thomson to serve as their secretary. Early in their initial meetings, an express rider arrived and reported that there had been fighting between British troops and Americans near Boston and that British cannons had begun firing at the city. The delegates viewed this report as an indication that a war with the mother country had started, and many were relieved to learn that the report was false. However, other delegates viewed the concern over the report as an indication that the colonies were ill-prepared to take up arms and that this issue needed to be addressed.

Congress then appointed a committee of 24, including Jay, to prepare a paper detailing the colonists' rights, their grievances with England, and proposals on addressing the problems. With both loyalists and those considered radicals like John Adams, the committee found it difficult to reach a consensus. Although Jay was generally considered a conservative, he sided with Adams during the committee debates. The problem of reaching an agreement was solved when Paul Revere arrived, carrying a copy of the Suffolk Resolves. The Resolves called on the people of Massachusetts to resist "the unparalleled usurpation of unconstitutional power" while at the same time affirming that King George was "our rightful sovereign." After a single day of debate, Congress unanimously approved the Resolves.

As a member of Congress, Jay also took part in the debates that led to the Continental Association. As detailed by Stahr, according to notes taken by John Adams, Jay took the position that "negotiation, suspension of commerce, and war are the only three things. War is by general consent to be waived at present. I am for negotiation and suspension of commerce." Thus, on October 20, 1774, Congress formed the Continental Association effective December 1, 1774, that prohibited both imports and exports with Great Britain, Ireland, and the British West Indies. Jay became one of the signers of the Association.

In April of 1775, Jay was once again one of the New Yorkers elected to represent his state at the Second Continental Congress. As relations between the colonies and England grew worse, he remained as one of the members of Congress who hoped to avoid war and reconcile with Great Britain. In May of 1776, Jay left Congress to spend time with his wife, who was ill, and with his father, who also suffered from poor health. During this time, he served as a member of New York's Provincial Congress. As a result, Jay was not in Philadelphia when Congress voted to approve the Declaration of Independence. Some question whether he would have supported the measure, but John Adams certainly was not one of them. On July 4, 1823, In Quincy, Massachusetts, Adams rose to offer a toast and said to, "the excellent President, Governor, Ambassador and Chief Justice, John Jay, whose name was not subscribed to the Declaration of Independence, as it ought to have been, for he was one of its ablest and faithful supporters."

When Adams called Jay an excellent president, he referred to his service as the President of Congress. Jay was elected to that position in the summer of 1778. During his tenure, Congress had problems due to a high turnover of delegates and their frequent absences. Nevertheless, Jay held this post for ten months, and during this period, he composed more than 500 letters on behalf of Congress. He also had the responsibility to meet with and entertain representatives from foreign countries.

Jay's time as President of Congress was a difficult one for him. According to his biographer, it has been called the "year of division." That same historian concludes that his greatest contribution may have been preventing a quarrelsome Congress from descending into chaos. Jay himself grew in the role. Through correspondence and by supporting the Commander in Chief, he had solidified a friendship with George Washington. In addition, his frustrations turned his thoughts to creating a strong national government. Finally, his knowledge about the views of the major members of Congress would aid him in the tasks he now undertook. First as his country's representative in Spain and then in Paris when he joined the American team whose job was to negotiate a peace treaty with England.

Jay and his wife Sarah set sail for Spain in late October 1779. Congress had given Jay the task of seeking recognition of the United States and hopefully an alliance against England as well as financial support from Spain for the new nation. Knowing he had little to offer the European country in return, he wrote Washington noting that the goals of his mission, "however just, will not be easily attained, and therefore its success will be precarious and probably partial." As it turned out, even these limited hopes proved to be unattainable. Spain refused to receive Jay as the Minister of the United States and declined to recognize American independence because of concerns that such recognition could ignite similar revolutions in their colonies. Nevertheless, Jay successfully obtained a $170,000 loan that the United States government pledged to repay. After this very modest success, he left Spain in May of 1782 and headed to Paris to join in the negotiations with England to end the Revolutionary War.

The American negotiating team included Jay, Benjamin Franklin, John Adams, and Henry Laurens. However, only Jay and Franklin were present in Paris; the other Americans would join them later. David Hartley and Richard Oswald represented England. Congress had directed the American team to keep the French government informed about the progress of the talks. Jay wrote a letter protesting this directive because he believed the Americans could achieve better terms without French involvement. Congress reversed their decision, and a treaty was negotiated with favorable terms for the United States. The Treaty of Paris was signed on September 3, 1783, and included British recognition of the United States as an independent nation and established boundaries that allowed the new country to expand westward. According to Arthur G. Sharp in his work, *Not Your Father's Founders*, the most surprised countries on hearing of the accord were France and Spain. John Adams gave Jay the bulk of the credit for the treaty saying he was "of more importance than any of the rest of us." Adams also noted that the French had bestowed on him the title of 'le Washington of the negotiation.' He called the description a flattering compliment to which he had not a right, saying it "belongs to Mr. Jay."

When Jay returned to New York in July of 1784, he learned that Congress had elected him to the post of Secretary of Foreign Affairs. As detailed by the historian Joseph Ellis in his book *The Quartet*, Jay set certain conditions for accepting the post. He required that he be free to appoint his staff, that he could speak as a representative of the confederation as a collective and (in the words of Ellis) "a rather audacious demand that the Congress move from its current location in Trenton to New York to facilitate his family obligations. It is a measure of Jay's prestige and the delegates' desperation that all the conditions he proposed were found acceptable."

In his new post, Jay sought to establish a strong American foreign policy. He prioritized establishing a stable American currency and paying off the country's Revolutionary War debt. He also worked to secure the recognition of the new nation by the established European powers. Jay also concerned himself with securing Newfoundland fishing rights and setting the country's borders under the best terms available at the time, and protecting American sailing ships from pirates. Unfortunately, his efforts were hampered by a Congress that was often absent or indecisive. Moreover, the country under the Articles of Confederation had neither an army nor a navy, so war may well have been disastrous. So, it may be said that his chief accomplishment when he left this post in 1789 was avoiding any such conflict.

When the Constitutional Convention was held in Philadelphia in 1787, Jay was blocked from joining the New York delegation by Governor George Clinton and his upstate supporters. By this time, Jay was known to be a proponent of a strong national government, which Clinton opposed. Jay had exhibited his preference for a strong executive branch as far back as 1777 when practically on his own he wrote the New York Constitution, which gave more authority to the executive than any other state constitution. As a result, the only member of the New York delegation who was a nationalist was Alexander Hamilton, who was certain to be outvoted by the other two New York delegates who opposed any changes to the Articles of Confederation.

After the convention produced the proposed Constitution, Jay took a leading role in supporting its ratification. He joined Hamilton and James Madison in writing *The Federalist Papers*. The papers were a series of 85 articles aimed at persuading reluctant New York state convention members to ratify the new Constitution. This would be a major task when New York chose its state delegates to consider the matter; only 19 of the 65 elected were known to favor ratification. Jay, of course, was one of them.

The convention met in Poughkeepsie, New York, and Jay proved to be a major force during the debates. Many of those opposed to the

Constitution called for its approval only with amendments that a second Constitutional Convention would be required to consider. Others supported ratification conditioned upon a right to secede from the union. A vote of 31 to 28 defeated the latter proposal.

Jay drafted a letter to address the question of amendments. The letter New York would send to the other states urged them to call another convention to consider proposed amendments. New York did propose amendments, but the state ratified the Constitution without making their adoption or consideration by a second convention a requirement. The vote to ratify was also a close one, 30 to 27. Jay proved successful in using both the carrot and the stick to sway those opposed to his side. The carrot being support for consideration of amendments to the Constitution and the stick being that New York City would secede and form its state if New York failed to ratify. Indeed, Jay's letter may well have been the driving force that resulted in New York joining the Union without conditions.

Once the Constitution had been ratified, it was obvious that George Washington would be the first president. When the president went about assembling his cabinet, he offered Jay the Secretary of State position. This post would have continued his role as Secretary of Foreign Affairs, and he declined the offer instead of accepting a position Washington called "the keystone of our political fabric" Chief Justice of the United States. Washington nominated Jay to the position on the same day he signed the Judiciary Act of 1789, which created the post. Two days later, Jay was unanimously confirmed by the United States Senate. The Jay court's main role was establishing the rules and procedures the court would follow. Jay himself did establish a precedent for the Supreme Court in 1790 when the Treasury Secretary and his old friend Alexander Hamilton wrote to the Chief Justice asking that the Court endorse legislation allowing the federal government to assume state debts. Jay responded that the Court could not endorse legislation, only rule on the constitutionality of cases brought before it. Jay's response predated Chief Justice Marshall's court ruling in the landmark case *Marbury v. Madison* by more than a decade.

In 1792 The Federalist Party nominated Jay as its candidate for Governor of New York. Jay received more votes than his opponent

George Clinton, but his majority was challenged based on vote technicalities in three counties that had delivered Jay his victory. Clinton supporters controlled the State legislature and the state courts, and as a result, enough Jay votes were disqualified to award Clinton the victory.

By the year 1794, the young United States of America was on the verge of another war with England. The former mother country blocked American exports, had failed to leave forts in the northern United States as called for by the Treaty of Paris, and seized American ships and supplies headed for France and impressing American sailors. President Washington gave Jay the task of negotiating a settlement with the English. In Jay's view, his country was totally unprepared for war. He negotiated what came to be known as the Jay Treaty, which ended British control of the northwestern forts but failed to address the country's concern relative to shipping rights and impressment. The emerging political party led by Thomas Jefferson, known as the Democratic-Republicans, denounced the treaty. In the House, James Madison and in the Senate, Aaron Burr, made speeches condemning it. The opposition to the treaty allowed Jay to joke that he could if he wished, make his way from one end of the country to the other by the light of his burning effigies.

Nevertheless, president Washington stood by the treaty, approved by the Senate 20–10, receiving exactly the two-thirds majority required for its adoption. In August of 1795, Washington signed the treaty, and given the fact that while attacking Jay could be done easily, the same was not true when it came to Washington. As a result, the criticisms of the treaty became more moderate in tone. In Jay's view, he had achieved his primary objective, avoiding a war the United States was ill-prepared to fight.

Having been defeated in a disputed election for Governor of New York in 1792, Jay was the obvious Federalist choice for that office in 1795. In May of that year, he was elected Governor, and he resigned as Chief Justice on June 29, 1795. He served as New York's Governor until 1801. His accomplishments as Governor included reforming the prison system, limiting the death penalty and abolishing flogging, constructing canals, and signing a bill that would gradually end slavery in the state.

Despite the measures he took as Governor and the fact that he was a founder of the New York Manumission Society, Jay's record of slavery is mixed. As late as the 1810 census, he is recorded as owning a slave.

John Jay (1745–1829)

He had over the years continued to purchase enslaved people and grant their freedom once he believed their work to "have afforded a reasonable retribution." Yet in the close 1792 election for Governor, his views on slavery cost him votes in upstate New York Dutch areas where slavery was very much practiced. Then in 1794, when he negotiated the Jay Treaty, he angered many southern Americans when he abandoned the demand for compensation for slaves who had been freed and transported to other areas by the British after the Revolution.

In 1801 Jay declined the Federalist nomination to run for another term as Governor. That same year President John Adams nominated Jay, and the Senate confirmed him to return to the Supreme Court as Chief Justice. But, again, Jay declined to serve, opting to retire from public

John Jay's grave.

life. Adam's then nominated John Marshall to the post and he became the man who shaped the modern Court and one of the most significant judges in the history of this country.

Jay retired to his farm in Westchester County, New York. His wife Sarah passed away shortly after that. Jay continued to enjoy good health, and with one very notable exception, he stayed out of the political arena. In 1819 he wrote a letter condemning Missouri's bid to enter the union as a slave state. He wrote that slavery "ought not to be introduced nor permitted in any of the new states."

On the evening of May 14, 1829, Jay suffered what probably was a stroke. He passed away three days later and was laid to rest per his wishes in what is known as the John Jay Cemetery in Rye, New York, only open to the public once a year. This is also the only Founder's cemetery protected by barbed wire.

For many years Jay was somewhat of a forgotten founder. Many people had heard of him, but few were aware of the depth of his accomplishments and contributions to the establishment of the United States of America. As the historian, Joseph Ellis has stated, "We can argue about who should be on the top of the list of most important founders until the cows come home, but it's clear he (Jay) should be part of the list."

Fencing with barbed wire protects the Jay Cemetery.

Rufus King
(1755–1827)

The Last Federalist Candidate for President

Buried at Old Episcopal Churchyard,
Jamaica, New York.

Military • Continental Congress • U.S. Constitution

This founder represented two states in his distinguished career. He served as a delegate from Massachusetts in the Continental Congress and in 1787 at the Constitutional Convention. After the ratification of the Constitution, he represented New York in the United States Senate. As a young man, he served in the Continental Army where, by a stroke of luck, he avoided losing a leg. He also served as the United States Minister to Great Britain twice. He was a candidate for national office in unsuccessful campaigns three times. His name was Rufus King.

King was born on March 24, 1755, in Scarborough, Massachusetts, a location that has since become part of the state of Maine. His mother was Isabella Bragdon, and his father was Richard King, a prosperous farmer-merchant and sea captain. This financial success created envy among some of his neighbors, and when rioting broke out after the Stamp Act of 1765, the King household was targeted by a mob that ransacked the house, destroying much of the furniture. King's father became a staunch Tory who again faced an angry mob at his home in 1774. One historian claims the latter event led to Richard King's death a year later and instilled in his son respect for order and reason.

Rufus King

At the age of twelve, King began his formal education at the Dummer Academy, today known as The Governor's Academy. He then attended Harvard College, and he graduated from that institution in 1777. He began to study law under Theophilus Parsons but suspended that study to join the militia and fight in the Revolutionary War. He served as an aide-de-camp under General Glover, who led a detachment to support a failed attempt to retake Rhode Island.

In his work *Rufus King and His Times*, Edward Hale Brush recounts an incident that occurred one morning when General Glover and his staff were seated around a table for breakfast. At one point, the firing of the British guns increased, and Glover sent King to investigate. King's seat at the gathering was taken by Colonel Henry Sherburne, who had scarcely seated himself when a cannonball entered through a window and smashed Sherburne's ankle resulting in the amputation of his leg. Later in life, Sherburne's and King's paths would occasionally cross, and King would remark that it was he who should be wearing a wooden leg.

After his time in the military, King returned to the study of law under Parsons. He was admitted to the bar in 1780, and he began his law practice in Newburyport, Massachusetts. In 1783 King was elected to the Massachusetts General Court. He then represented his state in the Continental Congress, serving from 1784 to 1787. At the time, he was one of the youngest members of that Congress. The Congress met in New York City where King met Mary Alsop, the daughter of John Alsop, a wealthy merchant and one of the New York delegates. The couple married on March 30, 1786. The Kings had seven children, five of whom survived to adulthood.

In 1787 King repressed Massachusetts at the Constitutional Convention in Philadelphia, a gathering he had opposed just a year before. At just 32 years of age, he had already earned the reputation of being a brainy legislator and a gifted orator. Although he arrived in Philadelphia opposed to changing the Articles of Confederation, his mind was changed as he listened to the issues being debated. In his work on the convention, the historian Clinton Rossiter described King as "an enthusiastic, sharp-witted, persuasive nationalist, who was the champion Committeeman of the summer."

King was fiercely opposed to slavery, and in the debates relative to how the Constitution would address that issue, he made those feelings clear when he lobbied to halt the spread of that institution in the country. His views made him extremely unpopular with the southern delegates. At least one southern delegate, William Pierce, who left the convention before its conclusion, did not share these views. Pierce described King as "much distinguished for his eloquence and great parliamentary talents," adding that King "ranked among the luminaries of the present age." King would sign the proposed Constitution and then campaign strongly for its ratification.

In 1788, at the urging of his good friend Alexander Hamilton, King closed his Massachusetts law practice and moved his family to New York City. He soon immersed himself in the state's politics, and in 1789 the New York legislature appointed him to be one of the state's original United States senators. As a senator, he was an ardent supporter of the economic policies proposed by the nation's first Secretary of the Treasury,

King Manor historic site.

the aforementioned Alexander Hamilton. He also supported the controversial treaty that John Jay had negotiated with Great Britain in 1795. The following year he resigned his senate post after being appointed the United States minister plenipotentiary to England by President Washington. He served in this position until 1803.

Upon returning to the United States, he became the Federalist Party candidate for vice president in the elections of 1804 and 1808. In 1804 the ticket of Thomas Jefferson and George Clinton crushed the Federalists in the electoral college 162–14. It was not much better four years later when James Madison and Clinton defeated Charles Pinckney and King by 122–47.

In 1812 King was once again appointed to the United States Senate, where he led the opposition to President Madison's handling of the War of 1812. Four years later, he was the last Federalist candidate for the Presidency, going up against James Monroe. In that contest, he won the electoral votes of just three states.

He returned to the Senate in 1820, where he strongly opposed the admission of Missouri to the union as a slave state. In a speech that year to an audience of whites and free blacks, he stated, "I have yet to learn that one man can make a slave of another. If one man cannot do so, no number of individuals can have any better right to do it." He lost

Rufus King (1755–1827)

the battle when the then Speaker of the House, Henry Clay, settled the dispute with the Missouri Compromise.

King remained in the Senate until 1825 when President John Quincy Adams appointed him to represent the United States in Great Britain once again. He served in that post for a year before ill health forced him to resign and return to the states. At this point, he had represented his country in Great Britain under four different presidents.

In 1827 he passed away at his estate, King Manor, located in Queens County, New York. His manor remains and is open to visitors on certain days. He was laid to rest not far from his home in the Grace Episcopal Cemetery. For more than thirty years, he served the nation as both a diplomat and a politician throughout his public life. He also came to be one of the leaders of one of the first two political parties to rise in the country after the Constitution's ratification.

The worn grave of Rufus King.

Francis Lewis
(1713–1802)

"All That Glitters Is Not Gold"

Trinity Church Cemetery
New York, New York

Declaration of Independence • Articles of Confederation

Francis Lewis was a Welsh-born merchant from New York City who was elected to the Continental Congress, where he signed the Declaration of Independence and the Articles of Confederation.

Lewis was born March 21, 1713, in the village of Llandaff, Glamorganshire, Wales, slightly northwest of the capital, Cardiff. He was the only child of Reverend Francis Lewis, an Anglican clergyman, and his wife, Amy (née Pettingal) Lewis, the daughter of an Anglican clergyman. Lewis was orphaned at age five and went to live with relatives, including a maternal aunt. He grew up in both Wales and Scotland and learned the Gaelic and Welsh languages. The Pettingal family, especially an uncle who was the dean at St. Paul's Cathedral, saw to his education at the prestigious Westminster School in London.

Upon graduation, Lewis became an apprentice at a mercantile business in London. When he turned 21, he inherited properties left by his father. He sold them and used the proceeds to start his own business in partnership with Edward Annesley. He acquired merchandise and sailed for New York City, arriving in 1734 or 1735. He left some of the goods

Francis Lewis (1713–1802)

Francis Lewis

with his partner in New York and took the rest to Philadelphia. There, he lived for two years before returning to New York.

Back in New York, Lewis was involved in the trans-Atlantic trade, making trips to several northern European ports, Saint Petersburg, Scotland, and Africa. Twice, he survived shipwrecks off the Irish coast. Circa 1743, Lewis broke up his business partnership with Annesley but married his sister, Elizabeth Annesley, on June 15, 1745. The couple had seven children, three of whom survived to adulthood:

- Ann Lewis (1748–1802) married Captain George Robertson (1742–1791) of the Royal Navy.
- Francis Lewis Jr. (1749–1814) served as churchwarden of St George's Parish in Flushing, New York, from 1791 to 1794. He married Elizabeth Ludlow (d. 1831), daughter of Gabriel Ludlow, Esq.
- Morgan Lewis (1754–1844) married Gertrude Livingston, the daughter of Judge Robert Livingston of Clermont. He was a governor and attorney general of New York.

NEW YORK PATRIOTS

In 1756, at the outbreak of the French and Indian War, Lewis supplied uniforms to the British. He was at Fort Oswego that August, delivering uniforms, when General Montcalm's forces and Indian allies attacked. Lewis was standing next to Colonel James Mercer, the fort's commander, when a cannonball killed him. The fort was surrendered to Montcalm, who permitted the natives to select thirty prisoners to keep or kill. Lewis was among them. While being tortured by his Indian captors, Lewis spoke in Welsh. The natives recognized similarities in the language and stopped and spoke with him. The chief then took Lewis to Montreal where he requested to return to his family. However, he was instead sent to France as a prisoner, where he remained until the end of the war.

In 1763, Lewis was exchanged and returned to New York. There, the British granted him 5,000 acres for his service. He re-established his mercantile business and quickly accumulated a large fortune, permitting him to retire at age 52 in 1765. The *Encyclopedia of American Wealth* estimated that his holdings ranked him fifth among all the signers of the Declaration.

In 1765, with the passage of The Stamp Act, Lewis turned against the British government. He was appointed to the Stamp Act Congress, held in New York. In 1877, granddaughter Julia Delafield wrote, "On October 25 [1765] they met for the last time, and had the honor of being the first body to pass the resolution that the colonies ought to be united and act in common. Among the members of the New York committee we find the names of Francis Lewis and Robert R. Livingston. This Congress had not in its ranks a more consistent and energetic opponent of the tyranny of the mother country than Lewis."

During the crisis, Lewis moved his business and family to Whitestone, now part of Flushing, Queens County, New York. In 1771, he moved the business back to New York City and, with his son, Francis Lewis Jr., became one of the leading merchants under the banner of Francis Lewis and Son. He also became a founding member of the Sons of Liberty there.

To protest the closing of the port of Boston in 1774, New Yorkers formed the Committee of Fifty to oversee the city. Lewis, by unanimous consent, became the 51st member on May 16. The committee eventually included sixty members who established the colony's new government.

Francis Lewis (1713–1802)

In 1775, sensing the risk of invasion, Lewis again moved the family and their belongings to Whitestone. He was elected to the Second Continental Congress on April 22, 1775, serving until November 19, 1779. He signed the Olive Branch Petition and used his own resources to help supply the army with clothing. On October 9, 1775, Lewis, John Alsop, and Philip Livingston were contracted by the Secret Committee of the Continental Congress to supply arms and ammunition. Benjamin Rush called Lewis "a very honest man and very useful in executive business."

When the vote for independence was called on July 2, 1776, New York's delegation abstained due to the lack of instructions from the provincial assembly. Thus, when independence was declared unanimously, 12 to 0, on July 4, New York was not among the colonies. Finally, the New York delegation received instructions to approve the measure, and Francis Lewis and the others signed the Declaration of Independence on August 2.

Only a few weeks later, on August 27, 1776, during the Battle of Brooklyn Heights, the British captured the Lewis estate at Whitestone. British Captain Birtch and a troop of light horsemen were sent to destroy the Lewis home. As the soldiers approached and a British warship opened fire on the house, Elizabeth remained calm. Thinking her shoe buckles were made of gold, a soldier bent down and tore them off.

"All that glitters is not gold," said Elizabeth to the young man. The buckles were just pinchbeck.

The soldiers ransacked the house, destroying books, papers, pictures, and furniture. They also took Elizabeth Lewis as a captive and imprisoned her without a bed or a change of clothes and little food.

Upon learning of this, General Washington ordered the arrest of two Loyalist women in Philadelphia and said these captives would receive the same treatment as Mrs. Lewis. Finally, an exchange was arranged, but Elizabeth's health was weakened.

That winter, while the troops were at Valley Forge, Lewis was a strong supporter of General Washington when the Conway Cabal became public. Meanwhile, in York, Pennsylvania, Lewis worked on the Articles of Confederation, which he signed in November 1778. He was just one of sixteen men to sign both the Declaration and the Articles.

He returned home in 1779 to be with his ailing wife. She passed in June 1779, and Lewis did not seek re-election after his term was up in November of that year. He then served as the chairman of the Continental Board of Admiralty until he retired from public service in 1781.

In his later years, from 1784 to 1786, Lewis was a vestryman at Trinity Church. He enjoyed the company of his family, especially his grandchildren. Lewis died on December 31, 1802, at age 89. He was buried in an unmarked grave at Trinity Church Cemetery in New York City. The descendants of the Signers of the Declaration of Independence added a granite marker and plaque in 1947.

Francis Lewis had many interesting descendants:

- His son Morgan served in the Continental Army during the Revolutionary War and later held many offices in New York, including governor (1804-1807). He was a major general in the War of 1812.
- Through Morgan, he was a grandfather of Margret Lewis (1780–1860), who married New York lawyer and politician Maturin Livingston and became parents to twelve children.
- Through his son Francis Jr., he was a grandfather of Gabriel Ludlow Lewis.
- Through his daughter Ann, he was a grandfather to Marianne Robertson (1779–1829), who married John Bird Sumner, the Archbishop of Canterbury and brother of Charles Richard Sumner, bishop of Winchester.
- Great-grandson Manny Livingston died at the Battle of Gettysburg during the Civil War.
- Great-great-great-grandson William A. Wellman was a Hollywood director.

Francis Lewis is also remembered in many ways:

- John Trumbull's 1819 painting *Declaration of Independence* includes Lewis, near Richard Stockton and John Witherspoon. This painting hangs in the Rotunda of the Capitol in Washington, D.C.

Francis Lewis (1713–1802)

- A granite boulder bears his name in the memorial park of the 55 signers near the Washington Monument in Washington, D.C.
- Francis Lewis High School and P.S. 79, "The Francis Lewis School" in Queens, New York, are named after Lewis.
- Francis Lewis Boulevard, known locally as "Franny Lew" or "Franny Lewie," stretches almost the entire north/south length of Queens.
- Francis Lewis Park is located under the Queens approach of the Bronx-Whitestone Bridge, on the site of the Lewis home.
- A society of the Children of the American Revolution located in Queens, New York, is named for him.
- A Masonic lodge, Francis Lewis #273, is in Whitestone.

Grave of Francis Lewis

Robert Livingston
(1746–1813)

The Chancellor

Buried at St. Paul's Episcopal Church Cemetery,
Tivoli, New York.

Continental Congress • Committee of Five • Diplomat

Robert Livingston played several roles in the founding of the United States. He was a very prominent political figure in New York, where he served as the first Chancellor of New York, which was then the state's highest judicial officer. He held that office for 24 years. He was elected to the Continental Congress and was appointed to the Committee of Five, charged with drafting the Declaration of Independence. He administered the oath of office to George Washington in 1789, served as Minister to France in the Jefferson Administration, and negotiated the Louisiana Purchase.

Livingston was born on November 27, 1746, in New York City, the eldest son of Judge Robert Livingston and Margaret Beekman Livingston. The Livingstons were rich land barons and heavily involved in the governing of the colony of New York. Young Robert entered King's College (now Columbia University) at the age of 15. There he met and became close friends with John Jay (see page 124). Amid the rumblings of rebellion, Robert graduated from King's College in 1765 and immediately entered a legal apprenticeship with his father's cousin and later governor

Robert Livingston (1746–1813)

Robert R. Livingston

of New Jersey, William Livingston. He was admitted to the bar in 1770 and that same year married Mary Stevens, the daughter of Continental Congressman John Stevens. He practiced law with John Jay and, in 1773, was appointed Recorder for New York City. He held that position until 1775, when his revolutionary sympathies made him unacceptable to the crown. He was immediately elected to the Continental Congress.

On June 11, 1776, Livingston became a member of the Committee of Five with Thomas Jefferson, Benjamin Franklin, John Adams, and Roger Sherman. They were tasked with drafting the Declaration of Independence. This appointment was seemingly a political maneuver designed to encourage New York into making a firm commitment to independence. Livingston felt that independence was desirable and inevitable but did not think that the time had yet come. Accordingly, he was one of the principal advocates of postponing the issue. He neither contributed to the draft nor signed the document.

The year 1777 was eventful for Livingston. He, John Jay, and Gouverneur Morris drafted New York's Constitution, which was submitted and approved. On July 30 of that year, he became the first Chancellor of New York, a position the new constitution had created and the highest judicial officer in the state. He held the position until 1777. That year, Livingston's home near Clermont, New York, was burned to the ground by the British Army under General John Burgoyne, in retribution for his siding with the Patriots. He rebuilt it between 1779 and 1782. The house is now a New York State Historic Site and a National Historic Landmark.

In 1781 Livingston became the Secretary of the Department of Foreign Affairs under the Articles of Confederation. During the two years he served in that position, he did all he could to strengthen America's alliance with France.

On April 30, 1789, Livingston, by being Chancellor of New York, administered the presidential oath of office to George Washington at Federal Hall in New York City, which was then the nation's capital. Washington appointed his friend, John Jay, to be Chief Justice of the Supreme Court. Alexander Hamilton was named Secretary of the Treasury. Despite Livingston's involvement, he was not rewarded with an office.

Perhaps for this reason and because he disagreed with Hamilton's federal assumption of state debts, Livingston turned anti-Federalist and entered a political alliance with members of the Jeffersonian opposition. In 1798 he ran for Governor of New York against John Jay, who had resigned from the Court, and lost. When Jefferson became President on March 4, 1801, he appointed Livingston the U.S. Minister to France. In that post until 1804, and aided by James Monroe's arrival, he negotiated the Louisiana Purchase, one of the country's greatest diplomatic coups. Overnight the size of the United States doubled. After signing the agreement on May 2, 1803, Livingston made this statement: "We have lived long, but this is the noblest work of our whole lives . . . the United States take rank this day among the first powers of the world."

During his time as U.S. Minister to France, Livingston met Robert Fulton. He developed the first viable steamboat, the *North River*

The tomb of Robert Livingston.

Steamboat of Clermont, whose home port was the Livingston family home in Clermont, New York. On her maiden voyage, she left New York City with him as a passenger, stopped briefly at Clermont, and continued up the Hudson River to Albany. The trip, which previously took nearly a week, was completed in just under 60 hours. In 1811 both men were appointed as members of the Erie Canal Commission funded by New York to explore a canal route to Lake Erie.

Robert Livingston died on February 26, 1813, a happy man having lived a full and successful life. He was buried in the Clermont Livingston vault at St. Paul's Church in Tivoli, New York. When the authors visited the grave, we were dismayed by the lack of memorialization at St. Paul's. There was no signage, no flag, no stone, nor any mention of his achievements or role in history. Today, both a bust in the United States Capitol and the name of New York's Masonic Library memorialize Robert Livingston as The Chancellor. Also, both Livingston County, Kentucky, and Livingston County, New York, are named for him.

William Livingston
(1723–1790)

"First Governor of New Jersey"

Buried at Green-Wood Cemetery,
Brooklyn, New York.

Continental Association • Governor • Constitution

William Livingston is best known as the first Governor of New Jersey following the Declaration of Independence. He was the brother of Philip Livingston, who signed that document. Livingston also served in the Continental Congress, where he signed the Continental Association. He was a delegate to the Constitutional Convention and signed the US Constitution.

Livingston, born November 30, 1723, in Albany, New York, was a son of Philip Livingston (1686–1749), the 2nd Lord of Livingston Manor, and his wife, Catherine (née Van Brugh) Livingston, the only child of Pieter Van Brugh, the Mayor of Albany. Livingston's siblings included Robert Livingston (1708–1790), the 3rd Lord of Livingston Manor; Peter Van Brugh Livingston (1710–1792), the Treasurer of New York; and Philip Livingston (1716–1778), a future signer of the Declaration of Independence.

Livingston was educated by tutors and in the local schools. When he was 13, he lived among the Iroquois in the Mohawk Valley with Henry Barclay, an Anglican missionary and Yale graduate. Livingston then enrolled at Yale at age 14 in 1737 and graduated in 1741, having

William Livingston

studied multiple languages and writing. Following his father's wishes, he next studied law under James Alexander in New York City and became his clerk. Alexander was the father of William Alexander, who became known as Lord Stirling and was a prominent major general during the Revolution. Livingston soon found himself bored with his law studies, and in the spring of 1746, he wrote an anonymous article attacking his boss's wife, Mary Spratt Provoost Alexander, a successful merchant. Alexander terminated the apprenticeship.

During this time, the young Livingston continued his writing and, in 1747, penned the pastoral poem "Philosophic Solitude, or the Choice of a Rural Life." This was one of the first successful poems by an American and was published many times by the 1800s.

Not deterred, Livingston's father found legal work for his son with William Smith, Sr., another leading attorney. Livingston studied with William Smith, Jr., and was admitted to the New York bar in 1748. He then set up a practice in New York City and Albany.

Livingston married Susannah French, the daughter of Philip French III and Susanna (née Brockholst) French, in 1748. The couple had 13 children, seven of whom lived to adulthood. Livingston also developed business associations with William Alexander, Lord Stirling, and John Morin Scott, a future Continental Congressman.

In 1752, Livingston was appointed by the New York colonial legislature to publish a history of the statutes enacted since the colony's founding, entitled *Digest of the Laws of the Colony, 1691–1751*. With partners William Smith, Jr., and John Morin Scott, he started a weekly journal, the *Independent Reflector*, the first New York newspaper to be critical of Catholic and Anglican Church activities in the New York City area. The three owners, Presbyterians, were called "The Triumvirate" by their contemporaries, who met weekly at The King's Arms tavern in an association dubbed The Whig Club, drinking to the memories of Oliver Cromwell and John Hampden. Their activities may have prevented the installation of an Anglican bishop in New York and diminished investment in King's College, which ultimately became Columbia University, founded by Anglicans. This put them at odds with New York Chief Justice James DeLancey, James Alexander, and Reverend Henry Barclay, Livingston's tutor.

The *Independent Reflector* only lasted until late 1753, after which Livingston published independent essays in the *New York Mercury* under the heading "The Watch Tower." These were early writings opposing a state-sanctioned church. King's College opened on October 31, 1754, and never appointed a bishop.

In 1754, Livingston was a commissioner working on the boundaries between New York and Massachusetts. He also helped to found the New York Society Library, which is still in existence. He then served briefly in the New York Provincial Assembly from 1759 to 1761, representing Livingston Manor in a rotation of family members through the office. In 1764, Livingston was back at negotiating boundaries, this time between New Jersey and New York. He was elected to the American Philosophical Society in 1768.

Livingston was back to writing history in 1770, releasing a history of the French and Indian War from the British perspective. In 1772, at age 49, he retired to New Jersey, moving to his wife's home in Elizabethtown. That winter, a fifteen-year-old Alexander Hamilton stayed with them while attending Francis Barber's grammar school. Livingston purchased land in Elizabethtown and started construction of a mansion dubbed Liberty Hall. It was completed in 1773 and stands to this day.

As tensions mounted with England, in December 1773, Livingston was among the Elizabethtown Committee of Correspondence, including Stephen Crane, John De Hart, William P. Smith, Elias Boudinot, and John Chetwood. On July 23, 1774, the New York legislature appointed Livingston to the First Continental Congress. There, he signed the Continental Association. He was then appointed to the Second Continental Congress, serving until June 1776, before the signing of the Declaration of Independence. Rather, he returned to New Jersey, which had declared its statehood and appointed Livingston as its first governor.

Livingston remained the governor of New Jersey for the rest of his life. During the early years immediately following independence, with the British headquartered in New York City, New Jersey was in a precarious position. Livingston dealt with Loyalists attempting to trade with the British and the regular movements of British troops through its borders. Between 1776 and 1779, Livingston moved his family to the Bowers-Livingston-Osborn House in Parsippany to stay away from British sympathizers and to avoid capture. There was a significant bounty on Livington's head, and the British frequently visited and looted Liberty Hall in his absence.

In June 1777, Livingston helped start a newspaper called the *New Jersey Gazette* that would be loyal to the cause. He then contributed to it with polemics and articles written under fourteen different pseudonyms. Scholars have dubbed him one of the most important propagandists in the colonies and certainly in New Jersey.

In June 1779, Loyalists raided the Parsippany home based on false information that Livingston would be there. Fortunately, he was not, and the perpetrators were captured. It is surmised a distant relative, the Loyalist mayor of New York City, David Mathews, was behind the attempt. The Livingstons returned to Liberty Hall later in 1779 and began restoring the property. In 1782, Livingston was honored to be a fellow of the American Academy of the Arts and Sciences.

In 1787, Livingston was elected to attend the Constitutional Convention on behalf of New Jersey. At 63, as one of the older delegates, his health limited his participation, but he did support the New Jersey

William Livingston (1723–1790)

Plan, which defended the representation of the smaller states. Livingston, along with David Brearly, William Paterson, and Jonathan Dayton, signed the Constitution on behalf of New Jersey. Livingston was asked, the following year, to be the Minister to the Netherlands, but he declined the position. He wrote a commentary (in French) comparing the government of England with the new US Constitution entitled *Examen du Gouvernement d'Angleterre comparé aux Constitutions des Etats-Unis*. At the outset of the French Revolution, Emmanuel-Joseph Sieyès cited Livingston's commentary in his pamphlet *What Is the Third Estate?*

The grave of William Livingston.

Susannah Livingston died in July 1789 and was initially buried in the Trinity Churchyard in lower Manhattan. Livingston "very much regretted" her passing, according to the local newspapers. Meanwhile, he oversaw the implementation of the new state and federal offices for New Jersey under the new US Constitution.

Livingston died in Elizabeth, New Jersey, on July 25, 1790. He was 66. Wrote the *Federal Gazette*, ". . . America bewails the loss of one of her most distinguished patriots . . ." Livingston was interred next to his wife at Trinity Churchyard in New York City. In 1844, both husband and wife were exhumed and moved to Green-Wood Cemetery in Brooklyn, New York.

William and Susannah's children included:

- Susannah Livingston (1748–1840) married John Cleves Symmes (1742–1814) and became the stepmother-in-law of President William Henry Harrison.
- Catherine Livingston (1751–1813) married Matthew Ridley (1746–1789) and later her cousin John Livingston (1750–1822), son of Robert Livingston.

NEW YORK PATRIOTS

- Mary Livingston (born 1753) married James Linn in May 1771.
- William Livingston Jr. (1754–1817) married Mary Lennington.
- Philip Van Brugh Livingston (born 1755) died unmarried.
- Sarah Livingston (1756–1802) was educated at home and raised to be politically aware, even serving as her father's secretary. At only 17, she married John Jay and accompanied him to Spain and Paris, where he helped negotiate the Treaty of Paris in 1783. Sarah is credited with writing the toast used to celebrate the treaty at the official dinner. Back in New York, Jay was appointed the Secretary of Foreign Affairs, and the couple established weekly diplomatic dinners in the new capital, New York City. She was also First Lady of New York when her husband was governor and then wife of the 1st Chief Justice of the Supreme Court.
- Henry Brockholst Livingston (1757–1823) was a lawyer who became a member of the US Supreme Court (1807–1823). He is buried in Green-Wood Cemetery.
- Judith Livingston (1758–1843) married John W. Watkins, an attorney.
- Philip French Livingston (1760–c. 1765) drowned in a boating accident in the Hackensack River.
- John Lawrence Livingston (1762–1781) died at sea aboard the USS *Saratoga*.

Other interesting descendants of William Livingston include:

- Julia Kean, the wife of Hamilton Fish, former Governor of New York and US Secretary of State.
- Thomas Kean, former Governor of New Jersey.
- Edwin Brockholst Livingston was a historian who focused on the Livingston family history.
- Henry Brockholst Ledyard, former Mayor of Detroit.

William Livingston is honored by the town of Livingston, New Jersey; Governor Livingston High School in Berkeley Heights, New Jersey; and the Livingston campus at Rutgers University.

Gouverneur Morris
(1752–1816)

The Penman of the Constitution

Buried at Saint Ann's Episcopal Churchyard,
Bronx, New York.

Articles of Confederation • U.S. Constitution • Military • Diplomat

He was a founding father who hailed from New York City. He argued with his family over the issue of American independence. He served in the army during the Revolutionary War. He signed both the Articles of Confederation and the United States Constitution. He is credited with writing large sections of the latter document including the preamble. He was also a United States Senator from 1800 to 1803. His name was Gouverneur Morris.

Morris was born on January 31, 1752, in what is now called the Bronx section of New York City at the family estate known as Morrisania Manor. As a boy, he exhibited a keen intellect. So keen in fact that, at the age of twelve, he enrolled in King's College which is now known as Columbia University. He began his studies in 1764 and graduated in four years. Since he was too young at age sixteen to start a career, he stayed at King's and received his Master's degree in 1771. Next Morris studied under the noted New York law scholar William Smith. It was through Smith, who opposed British tax policies in the colonies, that Morris met patriots such as John Jay and Alexander Hamilton.

NEW YORK PATRIOTS

Gouverneur Morris

In 1775, Morris was elected to the New York Provincial Congress. This Congress was organized by patriots who were seeking an alternative to the Province of New York Assembly, which was the official pro-British body. It was during his service in the Provincial Congress that Morris began supporting turning the colony of New York into an independent state. This put him at odds with both his family and his mentor William Smith who had turned away from the patriot cause when it moved towards pursuing independence.

When the Revolutionary War began, Morris favored reasoning with those Americans who stayed loyal to the king. This is hardly surprising since this group, known as Tories, included his mother and his half-brother. His mother gave the family estate to the British army to be used for military purposes. As the war went on, Morris changed his views on the treatment of Tories and favored tarring and feathering, whippings and the confiscation of property.

Gouverneur Morris (1752–1816)

In 1778, Morris was appointed to be a delegate to the Continental Congress. He was placed on a committee charged with reforming the Continental Army. Upon visiting the army at Valley Forge, he was so affected by the conditions that he became a spokesman for the military in Congress and was instrumental in reforms in training, methods, and financing. That same year, the Conway Cabal took place. Its purpose was to remove George Washington as Commander-in-Chief of the army. Morris cast the deciding vote that kept Washington in his job. In 1779, Morris was defeated in an election that cost him his seat in Congress. Most likely the defeat was caused by his support for a strong central government, a view not popular in New York at the time. After his defeat, he left New York and moved to Philadelphia.

In 1780, Morris shattered his left leg, and it had to be amputated. He said he had done it by getting his leg stuck in the spokes of a carriage he was driving. However, Morris had a reputation for having affairs with both married and unmarried women. There was gossip that the accident occurred while a jealous husband was chasing him.

In Philadelphia, he served as superintendent of finance from 1781 to 1785. He also worked as a merchant who put him in contact with the financier and founding father, Robert Morris (no relation). With the support of both George Washington and Robert Morris, he was appointed to be a Pennsylvania delegate to the 1787 Constitutional Convention.

Morris certainly made his presence known at the Convention. According to Catherine Drinker Bowen in her book *Miracle at Philadelphia*, Morris has been described as the most brilliant man at the Convention. She noted that he often spoke, giving 173 speeches, while never saying anything foolish or tedious. She describes his tactics as abrupt, first an eloquent explosive expression of his position and then cynically waiting for the Convention to catch up with him. He continued to favor a strong central government. He said, "When the powers of the national government clash with the states, only then must the states yield." Many others at the Convention, including Washington, shared his desire for a strong central government. Morris served on the Committee of Style and Arrangement who drafted the final language of the proposed constitution. Bowen called Morris the Committee's "amanuensis" meaning that he was responsible for most of the draft, as well as its final form. Also, Morris was one of the few delegates at the convention who spoke openly against slavery. According to James Madison's notes, Morris attacked slavery calling it a nefarious institution. After the Constitution was adopted, Morris was proud to put his signature on it. He then moved back to New York.

Morris went to France on business in 1789. He would not return for a decade. He served as Minister Plenipotentiary to France from 1792 to 1794. His diaries from this period have become a valuable resource concerning the French Revolution. They also help to document his ongoing affairs with women. He was openly critical of the French Revolution which led to a request from the French government to recall him which the United States eventually did.

Upon his return to the States, he resumed his law practice and entered politics. In 1800 he was elected to the United States Senate as a Federalist representing New York. He would serve until 1803. During this time, he championed improving transportation from the eastern part of the country to the interior. After being defeated in his reelection bid, he became Chairman of the Erie Canal Commission from 1810 to 1813. The canal was instrumental in transforming New York into a financial capital. That much was clear to Morris when he said: "The proudest empire in Europe is but a bubble compared to what America will be, must be, in the course of two centuries, perhaps of one."

Morris married at the age of 57. His wife was Ann Cary Randolph, the sister of Thomas Mann Randolph who was the husband of Thomas Jefferson's daughter Martha. Morris and his wife had one son, Gouverneur Morris Jr., who became a railroad executive.

On November 16, 1816, Morris passed away after causing himself internal injuries while using a piece of whalebone to clear a blockage in his urinary tract. He was laid to rest in Saint Ann's Episcopal Churchyard Cemetery along with his brother Lewis Morris who signed the Declaration of Independence.

Morris's grandson, William Walton Morris, a graduate of West Point, was a brevet Major General during the Civil War. He is also buried at Saint Ann's.

Gouverneur Morris (1752–1816)

Monument to Morris in the Bronx. His grave is beneath the church nearby.

During the early twentieth century, a great-grandson, also named Gouverneur Morris (1876–1953), authored novels and short stories. The Lon Chaney film *The Penalty* (1920) was adapted from one of them.

Morris was a substantial landowner in St. Lawrence County in upstate New York. There, the town and village of Gouverneur are named for him. During World War II, the liberty ship S.S. *Gouverneur Morris* was named after him.

In *Pennsylvania History* in July 1938, Philip Wild summed up Morris's life:

> Endowed with all that aids a man to achieve much for the common good, namely sterling character, wisdom, worthwhile place and wealth, Morris, on the contrary, chose to use these gifts to advance and strengthen the position of the small group of property men to which he belonged, instead of setting for his goal, the securing of the greatest good for all the people. His narrow conservatism led to his failure to secure political gifts from the people about whom he so often manifested his lack of faith. Lacking political backing, Morris became embittered and adopted positions which have brought rather caustic criticisms to him from historians. But it must be remembered that in public office, his efforts controlled as they were by the more liberal tendencies of his higher officers, produced much of significance for the United States.

Lewis Morris III
(1726–1798)

"The Last Lord of Morrisania"

Buried at St. Ann's Church of Morrisania,
Bronx, New York.

Declaration of Independence

Lewis Morris was a wealthy landowner in what is now Bronx County, New York. As a Continental Congressman from New York, he signed the Declaration of Independence. He was the older half-brother of Gouverneur Morris and the last "Lord of Morrisania Manor."

Morris, born April 8, 1726, at the family's estate, Morrisania (now part of Bronx County), New York, was the oldest son of Lewis Morris II (1698-1762) and his wife, Katrintje (née Staats) Morris. Morris had two brothers, Staats Long Morris (1728-1800) and Richard Morris (1730-1810). After his mother died in 1731, his father married Sarah Gouverneur (1714-1786). Half-siblings Mary Lawrence, Gouverneur Morris (1752-1816), Isabella, and Catherine were issues of this marriage. Morris was the nephew of Robert Hunter Morris (1700-1764), the colonial governor of Pennsylvania. He was also the cousin, by marriage, of New Jersey Governor William Paterson and father-in-law of New York Lieutenant Governor Stephen Van Rensselaer, the brother of Albany Mayor Philip Schuyler Van Rensselaer. General Anthony Walton White of the Continental Army was also a cousin, the son of his aunt Elizabeth.

Lewis Morris III

Morrisania had its origins with Morris's great-grandfather, Richard Morris, who came to New York via Barbados following the restoration of Charles II after the English Civil War. Richard, who had been in Cromwell's rebel army, purchased over 2,000 acres that are now within Bronx County, New York. His son, Lewis I, inherited and expanded the estate. Lewis I, the first royal governor of New Jersey, was very popular. Morristown, New Jersey, was named in his honor. His eldest son, Lewis II, was, for a time, the Speaker of the New York Assembly.

Lewis Morris III was educated by private tutors before attending Yale College. He graduated with an A.B. degree in 1746. That same year, following the death of his grandfather, his father became "Lord of Morrisania Manor." Young Morris returned from Yale to assist in the running of the estate. He married Mary Walton on September 24, 1749. The couple eventually had ten children:

- Catherine Morris (1751–1835) married Thomas Lawrence (1744–1823).
- Mary Morris (1752–1776).
- Colonel Lewis V. Morris (1754–1824) married Ann B. Elliott (1762–1848), sister-in-law of Congressman Daniel Huger.
- General Jacob Morris (1755–1844) married Mary Cox (1758–1827) (Morris, New York, is named after him).
- Sarah Morris (born in 1757) died young.
- Lieutenant William Walton Morris (1760–1832), aide-de-camp to General Anthony Wayne, married Sarah Carpender.
- Helena Magdalena Morris (1762–1840) married John Rutherfurd (1760–1840), a Senator from New Jersey.
- James Morris (1764–1827) married Helen Van Cortlandt (1768–1812), daughter of Augustus Van Cortlandt and granddaughter of Frederick Van Cortlandt.
- Captain Staats Morris (1765–1826) married Everarda van Braam Houckgeest (1765–1816), the daughter of Andreas van Braam Houckgeest and Baroness Catharina C.G. van Reeds van Oudtshoorn.
- Captain Richard Valentine Morris (1768–1815) married Anne Walton (1773–1858).

Morris was named as a judge of the Court of Admiralty, which oversaw shipping matters, in 1760. Upon the death of his father in 1762, Morris inherited the bulk of the family estate, becoming the third and final "Lord of Morrisania Manor."

Given his newfound wealth and influence, Morris was elected to the New York General Assembly in 1769 as part of the Livingston/DeLancey feud for power in the state. Morris was allied with his brother Richard, who was loyal to the Livingstons. Morris only lasted one term.

As tensions increased with Britain, he resigned from the Admiralty Court in 1774. In March 1775, countering the DeLanceys' power in the General Assembly, Morris led the call for a new Provincial Assembly, its purpose to elect delegates to the Continental Congress. Despite strong resistance, the meeting was held in White Plains on April 1. The elections were held on April 22 to select the delegates. Lewis Morris was one of them, serving until April 18, 1777.

While in Congress, Morris signed the open letter to the King of England. He was also involved in negotiations with the "Western Indians" in Virginia and was the chairman of the committee involved with financing and supplying the army. In 1776, Morris signed the Declaration of Independence. According to Howard Caine's 1972 film *1776*, based on the 1969 Broadway musical, Lewis, as chairman of the New York delegation, was reluctant to agree to anything because the New York Provincial Congress did not provide any instructions. When Morris learns of the destruction of his estates by the British from George Washington, he decides to sign the Declaration. In reality, when his brother General Staats Morris, who was in the British army, warned of the consequences of signing, Morris said, "Damn the consequences. Give me the pen." Within months, the British invaded Long Island and New York. Morrisania was looted and burned.

At the end of his term in 1777, Morris returned to Westchester, New York, and served as a county judge and New York State Senator until July 1, 1781.

After the war, he returned to Morrisania and began rebuilding it. He returned to the New York State Senate in 1783 and served until 1790. In 1784, he was made an honorary member of the New York Society of Cincinnati and appointed to the Board of Regents of the University of the State of New York.

In 1787, his half-brother Gouverneur Morris signed the Constitution after being credited with writing much of it. Morris then backed the Constitution in the New York ratifying convention, pushing for its narrow passage, 30 to 27. This pair of brothers are the only two brothers to sign both key founding documents, the Declaration and the Constitution.

In 1790, Morris offered Morrisania as the site of the new U.S. capital, replacing Philadelphia. Manhattan was chosen instead until Washington, D.C., was founded. In 1796, Morris was a presidential elector, voting for John Adams and Charles Cotesworth Pinckney.

According to the historian James J. Kirschke, by the end of Morris's life, Morrisania was in a 'leaky and ruinous' condition. "The estate house,

Lewis Morris III (1726–1798)

Grave of Lewis Morris III

servants' quarters, and grounds . . . had been used by the British as a horse park through most of the Revolution. An attack by the Continentals late in the war had caused further extensive damage. And Lewis had been too ill in the last several years of his life to manage and restore the place." Morris died at Morrisania on January 22, 1798, at age 71. He was buried in the Morris vault on the former Morrisania, now St. Ann's Church in the Bronx. His half-brother Gouverneur also rests there.

Some of Morris's noteworthy descendants include:

- Through his eldest son, Lewis V. Morris, he was grandfather to Lewis Morris (1785–1863), the father of Charles Manigault Morris (1820–1895), a Confederate officer.
- Also, through Lewis V. Morris, granddaughter Sabina Elliott Morris (1789–1857) married her first cousin, Robert Walter Rutherfurd (1788–1852), the son of John Rutherfurd and Helena Morris, and was the mother of Lewis Morris Rutherfurd (1816–1892), a pioneering astrophotographer who took the first

telescopic photographs of the moon and sun, as well as many stars and planets.
- Through his son, Staats Morris, his great-grandson was Daniel François van Braam Morris (b. 1840), a Dutchman and governor of Celebes in the Dutch East Indies.
- A great-granddaughter of his grandfather, Lewis Morris, named Mary Antill, was married to Gerrit G. Lansing, himself a brother of Congressman John Lansing. John Lansing's daughter, Sarah, was married to Edward Livingston, a great-grandson of Philip Livingston.

Thomas Paine
(1737 – 1809)

"The Mouthpiece of the American Revolution"

Buried at The Thomas Paine Gravesite (now empty),
New Rochelle, New York.

Thought Leader

Thomas Paine was a brilliant writer, political thinker, and opportunist. He became famous in the American colonies for his work *Common Sense*, which solidified public resolve regarding the American Revolution. He may have assisted in the drafting of the Declaration of Independence and later was involved in diplomatic efforts. His involvement in the French Revolution following his authorship of *Rights of Man* made him a man without a country despite its profound influences. Also, the architect of a single-span bridge, Paine burned the bridges of all his acquaintances and friendships throughout his later years, especially with his Deist work *The Age of Reason*. Always struggling with finances, Paine died a poor alcoholic in New Rochelle, New York. In later years, his bones were exhumed and subsequently taken to England and lost.

Paine, born January 28, 1737, in Thetford, Norfolk, England, was one of two children of Joseph Pain, a tenant farmer, and his wife, Frances (née Cocke) Pain. The elder Pain was also a staymaker (corset maker) who struggled with finances and an unhappy marriage. Mrs. Pain was the daughter of an attorney and town clerk who, according to an early Paine

Thomas Paine

biographer, had a "sour temper and eccentric character." Paine's younger sister, Elizabeth, born a year later, died in infancy.

Paine attended Thetford Grammar School until he was 13, at which point he became a tailor's apprentice assisting his father. At 19, during the Seven Years War, he served aboard the British privateer *King of Prussia*. Afterward, he settled in Sandwich, County Kent, where he established a shop as a staymaker. He married Mary Lambert on September 27, 1759, but his business soon failed. The struggling couple, now expecting, moved to Margate. Sadly, Mary went into early labor, and both mother and child died.

Paine returned to Thetford and worked in temporary roles while also continuing his staymaking. In December 1762, he became an excise officer in Grantham, Lincolnshire, transferring to Alford in August 1764. On August 27, 1765, he was dismissed for "claiming to have inspected goods he did not inspect." A year later, he requested reinstatement, which was granted. In 1767, he transferred to Grampound, Cornwall, and then asked to leave the post, pending a vacancy, and became a schoolteacher in London. Next, on February 19, 1768, he was assigned to Lewes, Sussex, where he lived above the tobacco shop of Samuel and Esther Ollive.

Thomas Paine (1737–1809)

Paine became involved in civic matters and the church vestry. On March 26, 1771, he married Elizabeth Ollive, the daughter of the late tobacconist. Paine subsequently took over the shop.

During 1772 and 1773, Paine lobbied Parliament on behalf of fellow excise officers for better pay and working conditions. In the summer of 1772, he published *The Case of the Officers of Excise*, and spent the following winter distributing 4,000 copies around London. In the spring of 1774, he was dismissed from the excise service due to his absence. Around this time, the tobacco shop also failed, and on April 14, he sold his household possessions to avoid debtors' prison. On June 4, 1774, he separated from his wife and moved to London. That September, the Commissioner of the Excise, George Lewis Scott, who was also a mathematician and Fellow of the Royal Society, introduced Paine to Benjamin Franklin. Franklin, the publisher of *The Pennsylvania Gazette*, the largest newspaper in America, suggested that Paine emigrate to America and gave him a letter of recommendation to his son-in-law, Richard Bache. Paine left the next month, but the voyage was difficult. The drinking water on the ship was bad, and five passengers died from typhus. When Paine arrived in Philadelphia on November 30, 1774, he was too sick to disembark. Benjamin Franklin's doctor carried him from the ship and cared for him for six weeks until he recovered. Back on his feet, Paine took an oath to become a citizen of Pennsylvania.

He soon began writing for Robert Aitken's *Pennsylvania Magazine* and was elevated to editor in March 1775. On March 8, 1775, the magazine published an unsigned abolitionist essay describing slavery as "execrable commerce" and an "outrage against Humanity and Justice." Benjamin Rush later assigned the authorship to Paine, who had reacted to seeing black slaves for the first time.

Though Aitken had intended the magazine to be apolitical, Paine brought a revolutionary perspective, writing in his first issue: "Every heart and hand seem to be engaged in the interesting struggle for American Liberty." Readership soared, especially among the working class.

In January 1776, Paine penned his seminal work *Common Sense*, which he signed anonymously 'by an Englishman.' In it, he made the case for American independence in strong prose and easy-to-understand language. Historian Danae Brack described it as "Perhaps the most significant example of protest rhetoric in American history." Word of the pamphlet spread rapidly, and soon, it was being printed, sold, and read in taverns everywhere. Some estimate over 100,000 copies were sold initially, and over the course of the Revolution, nearly a half million, including unauthorized copies. Unlike earlier works which criticized Parliament and remained respectful of the crown, Paine attacked the king and the monarchy.

Loyalists mounted a counterattack on *Common Sense*. James Chalmers of Maryland, in *Plain Truth* (1776), called Paine a "political quack." John Adams disagreed with Paine, publishing his *Thoughts on Government* (1776), where he argued for a more conservative approach to republicanism than radical democracy. Adams did not want the landless rabble to vote or hold office. Later in life, he referred to Paine's work as a "crapulous mass." Regardless, the public was motivated, and many enlisted in the cause. Historian Robert Middlekauff recognized that Paine successfully played on the religious sentiments of the public following the First Great Awakening by pointing out all the debauchery and tyranny associated with the various kings in the Old Testament. These feelings crossed denominations and brought unity in purpose.

Later that spring, the Second Continental Congress was in Philadelphia, deciding upon the course to be taken. Paine was definitely in town at the time and may have been consulted regarding the text of the Declaration of Independence, which was being conceived by the Committee of Five, including Thomas Jefferson, Ben Franklin, John Adams, Roger Sherman, and Robert R. Livingston. One of the early working drafts known as the Sherman Copy contained a statement on the back "A beginning perhaps—Original with Jefferson—Copied from Original with T.P.'s permission." Adams had hastily made this copy and noted the provenance. Some scholars, including the Thomas Paine National Historical Association, believe T.P. referred to Thomas Paine, though there is no official record of his involvement.

During July 1776, Paine served as a secretary for General Daniel Roberdeau in the militia known as the "flying camp" from Maryland, New Jersey, and Pennsylvania. At Fort Lee, New Jersey, Paine became the aide-de-camp for General Nathanael Greene, who then wintered at Brunswick, New Jersey. Faced with desertions and declining morale,

Thomas Paine (1737–1809)

Paine wrote *The American Crisis* to try to improve morale. The first article appeared in *The Pennsylvania Journal* on December 23, 1776:

> These are the times that try men's souls. The summer soldier and the sunshine patriot will, in this crisis, shrink from the service of their country; but he that stands by it now, deserves the love and thanks of man and woman. Tyranny, like hell, is not easily conquered; yet we have this consolation with us, that the harder the conflict, the more glorious the triumph. What we obtain too cheap, we esteem too lightly: it is dearness only that gives every thing [*sic*] its value . . .

Paine continued to write articles updating *The Crisis* until the end of the war.

In 1777, the Continental Congress, with Henry Laurens as President, named Paine the secretary to the Committee for Foreign Affairs, even though he was not a member. During this time, he became embroiled in a scandal involving Silas Deane, who was Congress's commercial agent in Europe, and the family of Robert Morris, the financier. Paine had letters printed in the newspapers accusing Deane of war profiteering. Upon further investigation by Congress, Deane was exonerated, and Paine was removed from his role as secretary in January 1779.

Out of work, Paine struggled to make ends meet. He worked as a clerk in a merchant office and as an auditor of the financial affairs of Robert Morris. In late 1779, he was named a clerk in the Pennsylvania Assembly. The next year, he had an idea for a national bank and put in $500 of his own money. This later became the Bank of North America. Paine wrote about the benefits of banking in *Public Good* (1780). He also criticized the land speculation in the West, saying the additional lands won should be under the control of the government rather than in private hands. This rankled land speculators such as George Washington and other Virginians. Later, the Northwest Territory largely followed Paine's model.

After Henry Laurens was President of Congress, he became involved in diplomacy and was imprisoned in the Tower of London by the British. Laurens' son, Colonel John Laurens, hired Paine to serve as his secretary while he was a special envoy to France. They departed in early 1781 and were successful in securing additional funds in Europe and also the release of the elder Laurens. During this time, Paine wrote about possibly bringing the American Revolution to England.

At the end of the war, Paine was again out of work and needed money despite his books selling well. He was granted $3000 from the Continental Congress. $500 from Pennsylvania, and New York gave him a small farm in New Rochelle that had been seized from Loyalists. Paine was not asked to play any role in the new government and instead investigated the viability of smokeless candles and a single-span bridge across the Schuylkill River. He was admitted to the American Philosophical Society in 1785.

In 1787, nearly destitute and disillusioned, Paine returned to England to try to raise funds for his bridge idea and to apply for a patent. Meanwhile, the French Revolution was underway and drew his attention. He began to write in favor of it, countering the writings of Edmund Burke. In 1792, Paine wrote *Rights of Man*, a rant against monarchy. The English decided to crack down on Paine for his revolutionary rhetoric, fearing the French Revolution could come to England. They sued Paine for seditious libel and tried to arrest him, but he had already fled to France. Said Paine at the time:

> If, to expose the fraud and imposition of monarchy . . . to promote universal peace, civilization, and commerce, and to break the chains of political superstition, and raise degraded man to his proper rank; if these things be libellous . . . let the name of libeller be engraved on my tomb."

He was tried in absentia, and lost.

In August 1792, despite not speaking the language, Paine became a citizen of France and was elected to the National Convention. However, Paine soon fell into disfavor when he argued against the execution of King Louis XVI, instead suggesting he should exiled to America. Robespierre, the head of the Committee of Public Safety, called for Paine's arrest, which happened on December 27, 1793. While imprisoned, Paine was to be executed. One night, the guard came through, marking with chalk the doors of those to be decapitated. Paine's door was marked, but because it was open while he was accepting visitors, the inside was marked rather than the outside. Thus, when the executioner later walked past Paine's closed cell, he was spared.

Paine remained in prison in Luxembourg until November 4, 1794, when James Monroe, the new minister to France, vouched for Paine. During his time in prison, Paine had written *The Age of Reason*, his treatise against religion, which was published in two parts in 1794 and 1795. He also penned, in 1795, his *Dissertation on First-Principles of Government*, in which he imagined a more just society, including concepts such as old-age pensions similar to modern Social Security.

In 1796, Paine penned a bitter letter to George Washington, who did not respond because Monroe diverted it. Paine felt Washington had allowed him to be imprisoned in France unjustly. So, Paine published the letter in the newspapers. He called Washington an incompetent general and a hypocrite.

Also, in 1796, Paine finally received a patent in England for his single-span bridge.

In 1798, Paine further explained his personal Deism in *Atheism Refuted; In a Discourse to Prove the Existence of a God*. However, Paine found more critics and fewer fans as time passed.

In 1800, Paine met Napolean, who claimed he had a copy of *Rights of Man* under his pillow. However, when Napolean moved towards monarchy, Paine called him "the completest charlatan that ever existed."

In 1802, at the invitation of Thomas Jefferson, Paine returned from France to his estate in New Rochelle, New York. Unfortunately, he turned to drink, having alienated nearly everyone who had supported him. Paine died in Manhattan on June 8, 1809. Only six people attended his funeral, as he was buried under a walnut tree on his farm after the Quakers refused to accept him in their cemetery. A rhyme from the period went:

> Poor Tom Paine! There he lies:
> Nobody laughs and nobody cries
> Where he has gone or how he fares
> Nobody knows and nobody cares!

In 1819, William Corbett, who intended to give Paine a heroic reburial in his native England, came to New Rochelle and exhumed Paine's bones. Unfortunately, when Corbett returned to England, he did not follow through and still had the bones among his effects when he died in 1834. There is no certainty about what happened to his remains after that. People have variously claimed to have his skull, jaw, right hand, and other bones.

The Thomas Paine Monument remains in New Rochelle, marking the site where he was originally buried. Nearby is his homestead, though the original house was replaced long ago. It is the site of the Thomas Paine Memorial Museum.

Statues of Paine can be found at Parc Montsouris, Paris; Morristown, New Jersey; and Thetford, England. He has been honored in many ways worldwide, and his writings are still studied as classics of political thought.

Monument of Thomas Paine

William Paterson
(1745–1806)

Author of the New Jersey Plan

Buried at Albany Rural Cemetery,
Menands, New York.

Signer of US Constitution • Governor • Senator • Supreme Court

William Paterson, born in Ireland, was a lawyer from New Jersey who was one of the most respected jurists of his era. Paterson was a signer of the US Constitution, a US Senator, Governor of New Jersey, and an Associate Justice on the US Supreme Court.

Paterson was born December 24, 1745, in County Antrim, Ireland, the son of Richard Paterson and his wife, Mary, both Ulster Protestants. The elder Paterson was a tin plate worker and traveling peddler of household goods. The family immigrated to New Castle, Pennsylvania, in 1747 but moved to New York and Connecticut before settling in Princeton, New Jersey. Here, Richard Paterson established a general store on the main road between New York and Philadelphia, across from Nassau Hall, later the site of Princeton University.

Young William grew up watching the university grow and expand across the street. The family's store catered to this increasing opportunity. But William wanted to be more than just a store clerk, and at age 14, in 1759, he was tested for his proficiency in Greek and Latin. He scored well enough to be admitted and studied the classics, history, political theory, and moral philosophy. Seeking to improve his character and gain

William Paterson

proficiency in eloquence and oratorial skill, he took additional classes towards a Master's degree, awarded in 1766. After he graduated, he next read law with Richard Stockton, one of the best-known attorneys in colonial America, and earned admission to the bar in 1768.

Paterson then moved to New Bromley, in Hunterdon County, New Jersey, and opened a law practice. However, he struggled mightily, and after moving around a few times, found himself keeping store with his brother at his mercantile business in Princeton. Then, his father went bankrupt in 1775. It could not have been timelier.

As hostilities increased with England, Paterson became involved in the Patriot cause. Starting in May 1775, he served as a delegate to the First Provisional Congress of New Jersey. As the assistant secretary of the convention, he assisted in the drafting of the New Jersey constitution.

After independence was declared in 1776, Paterson was appointed New Jersey's first attorney general, serving until 1783. During his tenure, he punished Loyalists. He also settled down at this time, purchasing a farm on the Raritan River in 1779. He constructed a home he dubbed "The Raritan" and married Cornelia Bell, the daughter of a wealthy landowner. A daughter, Cornelia Bell Paterson, was born in 1780.

On November 24, 1780, Paterson was elected to the Continental Congress by the New Jersey legislature, but he declined to take the seat and never served. He was concerned about being away from his wife and young children. A daughter, Frances, was born in 1782 but fell in and died in June 1783. That November, Cornelia gave birth to their son, William Bell Paterson, but she did not survive, dying four days later, on November 13, 1783. Paterson next married Euphemia White in 1784.

In 1787, Paterson, four years removed from his role as attorney general, was selected with Governor William Livingston, David Brearly, and Jonathan Dayton to represent New Jersey at the Constitutional Convention in Philadelphia. At five feet, two inches, Paterson was the smallest member of the convention, but that did not stop him from speaking out about the rights of the smaller states. He proposed what became known as the New Jersey Plan, calling for a unicameral legislative body with equal representation from each state. Said delegate William Pierce of Georgia:

> Mr. Patterson [sic] one of those kind of Men whose powers break in upon you, and create wonder and astonishment. He is a Man of great modesty, with looks that bespeak of no great extent—but he is a Classic, a Lawyer, and an Orator;—and of a disposition so favorable to his advancement that every one [sic] seemed ready to exalt him with their praises. He is very happy in the choice of time and manner of engaging in a debate, and never speaks but when he understands his subject well. This Gentleman is about 34 yrs of age, of a very low stature.

Paterson's notes from the convention were published in 1904 and show the evolution of some of the basic concepts of the Constitution from his perspective:

- Govr Randolph- Propositions founded upon republican Principles.
- The Articles of the Confdn should be so enlarged and corrected as to answer the Purposes of the Instn.
- That the Rights of Suffrage shall be ascertained by the Quantum of Property or Number of Souls—This the Basis upon which the larger States can assent to any Reform. Objn - Sovereignty is an integral Thing— We ought to be one Nation.
- That the national Legr should consist of two Branches.
- That the Members of the first Branch should be elected by the People, etc. This the democratick [sic] Branch—Perhaps, if inconvenient, may be elected by the several Legrs.
- Members of the 2nd Branch to be elected out of the first—to continue for a certain Length of Time, etc. To be elected by Electors appointed for that Purpose.
- The Powers to be vested in the national Legr—A negative upon particular acts, etc. contravening the Articles of the Union—Force.
- A national Executive to be elected by the national Legr.

Of course, following the Great Compromise, the Constitution included both the House of Representatives and the Senate. Following Paterson from his New Jersey Plan and then his notes indicate his creative and compromising nature. Paterson was one of the delegates to sign the Constitution from New Jersey.

In 1789, Paterson, along with Jonathan Elmer, was one of the first senators from New Jersey, serving until 1790. As a member of the Senate Judiciary Committee, he helped draft the Judiciary Act of 1789, which established the federal court system. The first nine sections of this law are in his handwriting.

On November 13, 1790, following the death of his friend, Governor William Livingston of New Jersey, Paterson resigned from the Senate and succeeded him. He remained in the role until 1793, during which he helped review, organize, and codify English laws that were in use in New Jersey.

William Paterson (1745–1806)

Grave of William Paterson

On February 27, 1793, President George Washington chose Paterson to be an associate justice of the United States Supreme Court in the seat vacated by Thomas Johnson. Paterson accepted and resigned as governor of New Jersey. He then spent the last 13 years of his life devoted to building a stable and powerful federal judiciary. Several of the cases he decided laid important foundations for the doctrine of judicial review. He also presided over trials of several of the Whiskey Rebellion conspirators.

In 1795, Paterson declined to accept an appointment to succeed Edmund Randolph as Secretary of State. Instead, Timothy Pickering was selected, serving through the Adams administration. Paterson stayed on at the Supreme Court. He was the heir apparent when Chief Justice Oliver Ellsworth resigned in 1800, but John Adams, out of concern for his close ties to Alexander Hamilton, did not offer the position.

Paterson stayed connected to Princeton, helping to found, with Aaron Burr, the Cliosophic Society. He was elected to the American Philosophical Society in 1789 and as a Fellow of the American Academy of Arts and Sciences in 1801.

In 1803, Paterson was injured when his coach crashed. Following this, his health began to fail. He left New York City and headed to Albany to live with his daughter, Cornelia Paterson Van Rensselaer, the wife of Stephen Van Rensselaer. There, he died, on September 9, 1806, at 61.

Paterson was interred in the vault at the Van Rensselaer Manor House. However, when the home was demolished in 1900, his remains were exhumed and reburied at the Van Rensselaer plot at Albany Rural Cemetery in Menands, New York. There is also a cenotaph in his honor at the Van Liew Cemetery in New Brunswick, Middlesex County, New Jersey.

William Paterson University and the city of Paterson, New Jersey, are named after him.

Philip John Schuyler
(1733–1804)

Father-in-Law of Hamilton

Buried at Albany Rural Cemetery,
Menands, New York.

Military • Political

Philip John Schuyler is best known as the father of Elizabeth Schuyler, who married Alexander Hamilton, the military hero, Federalist, and first Secretary of the Treasury. Schuyler was also a major general during the American Revolution and served in the Continental Congress. After the Revolution, he was a senator from New York in the First Congress and later the Fifth Congress. He was also a wealthy landowner and state politician who encouraged the ratification of the US Constitution and was known for his high character and virtue.

Philip John Schuyler was born on November 22, 1733, in Menands, in Albany, New York, to Johannes Schuyler Jr., a merchant, and his wife, Cornelia (née Van Cortlandt) Schuyler. He was the eldest son and heir to the family estate. The family is believed to be connected to a Schuyler who settled in New York, emigrating from Amsterdam in the mid-1600s. They were wealthy and likely belonged to nobility since they were permitted to hang their coat of arms painted upon the local church's windows.

Schuyler's father died in 1741 when he was eight. He was then raised by his mother and grandfather, Johannes Sr., until his death in 1747.

Philip John Schuyler

Schuyler attended the public school in Albany and was then tutored at the Van Cortlandt family estate in New Rochelle. Next, he studied with a private tutor, Reverend Peter Strouppe, to learn French and mathematics to go with his Dutch and English fluency. During this time, Schuyler began to suffer from a debilitating illness, similar to gout and arthritis, that would plague him his entire life, often leaving him incapacitated.

Despite his illness, Schuyler was a successful businessman around Albany and interacted in the privileged social circles of his rank. His business interests involved trading with the Indians at Oswego, and he went on many trade missions before the French and Indian War. During this time, he learned to speak Mohawk.

During the French and Indian War, in 1755, Schuyler raised a company and was commissioned a captain thanks to his cousin James DeLancey, the lieutenant governor. Later that year, on September 7, 1755, he married Catherine Van Rensselaer of another well-to-do New

York Dutch family. Ultimately, they had fifteen children together, eight of whom lived to adulthood. Schuyler served under Colonel John Bradstreet as a quartermaster at Oswego until the fort fell. He also took part in the battles of Lake George and Oswego River. The following year, he had left the army and was elected to the common council in Albany as a local politician.

In 1758, Schuyler rejoined the army as a major and fought at the Battle of Fort Frontenac. He was then dispatched to England to represent New York regarding settling claims before the British government regarding his quartermaster role. He stayed in England until 1763 when he left the army again and returned home.

He then began constructing his home, known as Schuyler Mansion (now the General Schuyler House). He expanded his business interests to include a lumber concern in Saratoga, New York, and the first flaxseed mill in America. In 1768, he was elected to the New York Assembly, serving there until 1775. During this time, he came to oppose the colonial government and was made a colonel of the militia but was also limited by his chronic illness.

Schuyler was elected to the Continental Congress early in 1775, serving until he was selected as one of the four major generals for the Continental Army under George Washington on June 19. He was given command of the Northern Department and planned the Invasion of Canada but was unable to lead it due to his health failing while on Lake Champlain, on the way to Quebec. Richard Montgomery led the expedition in the field.

In 1777, when the British invaded New York following the failed Canada campaign, they targeted Fort Ticonderoga. After General St. Clair surrendered the fort, both he and Schuyler were court-martialed. In the meantime, Horatio Gates was given command of the Northern Department. This was not before Schuyler had written to advise Washington on handling the forces at Saratoga on his home turf. Some surmise that had Schuyler not advised Washington, Gates and Benedict Arnold might not have been victorious against the British there. Saratoga was a key victory for the Americans. Gates and Arnold were heroes, and Schuyler's home was burned to the ground during the campaign. The following year, Schuyler and St. Clair were acquitted. France, seeing the victory over the British, agreed to join in the fight.

Now no longer in command of the Northern Department and his name cleared, Schuyler left the army on April 19, 1779, and returned to the Continental Congress. He also began rebuilding his homestead. On December 18, 1780, his daughter Elizabeth married Alexander Hamilton before his heroism at Yorktown. In 1781, Schuyler was the target of a failed kidnapping plot. Fortunately, he was tipped off and managed to leave before the kidnappers arrived at his estate.

After the Revolution, Schuyler was one of the founding members of the New York Society of the Cincinnati. From 1780 to 1784, he was a member of the New York State Senate and Surveyor General from 1781 to 1784. He returned to the state senate from 1786 to 1790, supporting the US Constitution's passage. During these years, he expanded his estate near Saratoga to tens of thousands of acres and had many slaves and tenant farmers. He also owned mills, stores, and schooners on the Hudson River.

Upon the passage of the US Constitution, Schuyler was elected to the US Senate representing New York, along with Rufus King, in the First Congress. He served from July 27, 1789, to March 3, 1791. He lost a reelection bid to Aaron Burr in 1791 and returned to the state senate from 1792 to 1797. He was then elected to the US Senate, serving from March 4, 1797, until his resignation on January 3, 1798, due to his chronic illness.

Catherine Schuyler died in 1803, as the couple approached 48 years of marriage. This greatly affected Schuyler. After his son-in-law Alexander Hamilton was killed in a duel with Aaron Burr on July 12, 1804, Schuyler replied to the many letters of condolence. From one of them:

> My warmest and unfeigned acknowledgments are due to the President and members of the St. Andrew's Society, for the delicate and feeling manner in which, they have conducted with me on the irreparable loss I have sustained, in the death of a son, who had endeared himself to me, by the most tender solicitude; who was the kindest and most affectionate husband to my dear and distressed daughter . . .

Philip John Schuyler (1733–1804)

Four months later, Schuyler died in Albany on November 18, 1804, from his "lingering illness." Schuyler was buried in Albany Rural Cemetery in Menands, New York. A huge obelisk marks the grave.

One aspect of Schuyler's life that is hard to quantify is his influence in social circles, individually and through his family. He was selected as one of the four lieutenants to George Washington, indicating he was held in high regard by Washington and the Continental Congress. But it is his extended family that further indicates his impact. As discussed, his second daughter, Elizabeth, was the wife of Alexander Hamilton. Schuyler was very fond of his son-in-law, and the two were close. Schuyler's eldest daughter, Angelica, married John Barker Church, who was later a British MP. Daughter Margaret married Stephen Van Rensselaer III, the 8th Patroon of Rensselaerwyck, the estate of the Rensselaers. Son John married Elizabeth Van Rensselaer, Stephen's sister. Son Philip served in the US House of Representatives. Son Rensselaer married Elizabeth Ten Broeck, the daughter of General Abraham Ten Broeck. The younger children also married well.

Philip's cousin Peter commanded the Jersey Blues. Cousin Hester was married to William Colfax of Washington's Life Guards and later the general in charge of the Jersey Blues. His brother-in-law Dr. John Cochran was the Director-General of Military Hospitals for the Continental Army.

Schuyler's name has been used in honor of many places, especially in New York. There are the towns of Schuyler and Schuylerville. There is also Schuyler County in New York as well as Illinois and Missouri. Fort Schuyler was built at the tip of Throggs Neck in the Bronx and now houses the Maritime Industry Museum and the State University of New York Maritime College. The Philip Schuyler Achievement Academy is in Albany, New York, though a name change is soon expected due to his ownership of slaves.

Schuyler has appeared in works of art, including the painting of the *Surrender of General Burgoyne* by John Trumbull hanging in the US Capitol. A bronze statue by J. Massey Rhind was erected outside city hall in Albany in 1925. Due to Schuyler's ownership of slaves, Albany's mayor, in 2020, ordered the statue removed. The mayor of Schuylerville, New York, requested it the next day to be moved to Schuyler House, managed by the National Park Service. Schuyler is also depicted in the play *Hamilton* in a non-speaking role.

Impressive monument to Philip Schuyler.

Baron Friedrich Wilhelm von Steuben
(1730 – 1794)

The Prussian General

Buried at Steuben State Memorial Site,
Steuben, New York.

Military

Baron von Steuben was a Prussian military officer who became a major general and Inspector General of the Continental Army. He is credited with developing the military training and manual that greatly improved American troops' performance in the field. Later in the war, von Steuben served as Washington's chief of staff. Baron von Steuben was likely an openly gay man at a time when sodomy laws outlawed such behavior.

Friedrich Wilhelm August Heinrich Ferdinand von Steuben (born Friedrich Wilhelm Ludolf Gerhard Augustin von Steuben, later known as Baron von Steuben, was born on September 17, 1730, in Magdeburg, Kingdom of Prussia (now Germany), to Captain Wilhelm von Steuben, of the Royal Prussian Engineers, and his wife, Elizabeth von Jagvodin. His parents were Protestants, though Jesuits taught von Steuben. From a young age, he accompanied his father on military adventures and may have served at age 14 with his father during the War of the Austrian Succession.

Von Steuben officially joined the Prussian Army when he was 17. He was battle-tested right away and rose through the ranks quickly, from second lieutenant to first lieutenant, to captain. In 1762, he became

Friedrich Wilhelm von Steuben

an aide-de-camp to Frederick the Great and received personal training from the king. However, the following year, when the war ended, he was unemployed. Von Steuben later wrote that "an inconsiderate step and an implacable personal enemy" was the cause of his dismissal. Some historians have speculated he was removed because of his homosexuality. However, he carried with him the knowledge of the finest army in the world at that time, known for its discipline.

Over the next dozen years, von Steuben was the grand marshal of the kingdom of Hohenzollern-Hechingen. In 1771, he accompanied his prince to France and had been granted the title baron. However, Baron von Steuben, who had been born a commoner, was deeply in debt.

In 1777, Baron von Steuben traveled to France to meet with his connection there, the French Minister of War, Count de St. Germain

Baron Friedrich Wilhelm von Steuben (1730–1794)

and was introduced to Ben Franklin. A position in the Continental Army was discussed, but the Americans had become tired of foreign mercenaries who demanded high rank. Franklin told the baron he would have to come as a volunteer and present himself to Congress. Von Steuben left the meeting disappointed and returned to Prussia. Upon arriving, he found himself embroiled in a controversy, anonymously accused of having "taken familiarities" with young boys while in the service of the prince of Hohenzollern-Hechingen. The baron realized his potential for continuing his military career in Europe was likely ruined, though he was not prosecuted. Instead, he returned to Paris and took Franklin up on the offer. Franklin likely knew of the baron's alleged issues but overlooked them. Count de St. Germain vouched for the baron's abilities.

The French government paid Baron von Steuben's passage to America. On September 26, 1777, he, his dog Azor, his aide de camp, Louis de Pontiere, and his military secretary, Pierre Ettienne Duponceau, sailed for America, arriving in Portsmouth (now Maine), on December 1. Upon arrival, he was nearly arrested by the locals because they mistook his group's red Prussian uniforms for British. The party then traveled to Boston, where they were extravagantly entertained. They then traveled overland to York, Pennsylvania, where the Congress was seated, arriving on February 5, 1778.

Franklin's letter of introduction to George Washington and Congress was deliberately misleading, exaggerating his credentials. He was introduced as "His Excellency, Lieutenant General von Steuben, Apostle of Frederick the Great," despite von Steuben having been only a captain. In French, von Steuben's title in the Prussian Army was "Lieutenant General Quarters Maitre," which meant he was a quartermaster. Franklin embellished the translation to "Lieutenant General."

Not picking up on Franklin's ruse, Congress accepted the baron's offer to volunteer without pay, though they promised compensation after the war dependent on his contributions. He reported to George Washington at Valley Forge on February 23. Washington rode out to meet him but noticed his small entourage. He found it peculiar, and though he later learned the baron had only been a captain, he approved of him, "He appears to be much of a gentleman, and as far as I have had an opportunity of judging, a man of military knowledge, and acquainted with the world."

Baron von Steuben was a native German speaker and did not know English. Fortunately, he was fluent in French, as were several officers in Washington's camp. Washington's aide-de-camp, Alexander Hamilton, and Major General Nathanael Greene were instrumental in translating for the baron. Washington asked von Steuben to inspect the army and found them short of everything but spirit. He said, "no European army could have held together in such circumstances." He next set about to devise a training regimen.

Wrote one soldier about his first impression of the baron; he was "of the ancient fabled God of War . . . he seemed to me a perfect personification of Mars. The trappings of his horse, the enormous holsters of his pistols, his large size, and his strikingly martial aspect, all seemed to favor the idea. He turned the volunteers into a great army."

The baron worked on camp layouts and sanitation standards that would be used until the early 20th century. The men had been relieving themselves where convenient, and animal carcasses were left to rot nearby. Von Steuben brought order to this, creating quarters for the command center, offers, and soldiers, and placing kitchens and latrines on opposite sides. The latrines were placed downhill.

Impressed by what he had seen, Washington recommended to Congress that von Steuben be made the Continental Army's Inspector General. This was approved on May 5, 1778. Congress assigned the baron the rank and pay of major general. Von Steuben next focused on cleaning up the books regarding the procurement of supplies. He enforced the keeping of meticulous records and performed strict inspections. This eliminated the graft that had been commonplace.

Next, von Steuben focused on the soldiers. He selected 120 men to form an honor guard for George Washington and used them to demonstrate military training to the remaining troops. This train-the-trainer approach was very effective and included the use of bayonets. He wrote the orders in German, which were then translated to French, and then to English. The eccentric von Steuben was also loved and respected by the men as he drilled them twice a day in full military dress. The baron's

Baron Friedrich Wilhelm von Steuben (1730 – 1794)

use of profanity in several languages made him popular with the men. The training was changed to a process whereby new soldiers were trained gradually by their leaders in their regiments rather than just being assigned without traning.

During this period, the baron met Captain Benjamin Walker. Remarked von Steuben, "If I had seen an angel from Heaven, I should not have more rejoiced." Shortly after that, Walker was made the baron's aide-de-camp. It was the beginning of a lifelong relationship.

The baron also socialized with the troops. One of his aides, Pierre-Étienne Du Ponceau, recalled a wild party given at Valley Forge. "His aides invited a number of young officers to dine at our quarters," he wrote, "on condition that none should be admitted, that had on a whole pair of breeches." The men dined in torn clothing and, he implied, no clothing at all.

While homosexual relationships were common during this time, there was no concept of gay marriage or gay pride. There was no language to describe it and no open culture. It was a private matter, generally kept out of the public eye. Sodomy was a crime in many jurisdictions, but romantic relationships between men were tolerated until the 19th century. Only in the 20th century did the U.S. military crack down on homosexual behavior.

The positive impact of von Steuben's training was noticed in the subsequent battles at Barren Hill on May 20, 1778, and at Monmouth in June. At Stony Point, the army won based on von Steuben's bayonet training, their muskets unloaded. That winter, von Steuben's *Regulations for the Order and Discipline of the Troops of the United States*, also known as the "Blue Book," was completed based on the actions at Valley Forge. This book was used by the army until 1814 and impacted drills and tactics until the Mexican-American War in 1846.

After sitting on the court-martial of Major John André in 1780, von Steuben was assigned to Nathanael Greene for the Southern campaign. He was instrumental in Virginia's defense and led a division at the decisive Battle of Yorktown in 1781.

For the next two years, von Steuben moved to New York, to Washington's headquarters at Newburgh, until the army was demobilized.

He aided in planning the nation's defense and, in May 1783, presided over the founding of the Society of the Cincinnati. He was discharged from the military with honor on March 24, 1784.

After the war, the baron was made a U.S. citizen and settled in New York City with his companion, William North. He created a special room for him called the Louvre. Von Steuben also became a prominent figure and elder in the German Reformed Church and served as president of the German Society of the City of New York.

Von Steuben, who lived extravagantly, was out of money and petitioned Congress for more. He was granted properties confiscated from Loyalists in New Jersey. These and the New York City property were used to pay debts while the baron tempered his lifestyle while supporting Walker and North. He then moved to upstate New York, in Oneida County, near Rome, where he was granted a 16,000-acre estate. There, he lived with Walker and North. "We love him," North wrote, "and he deserves it for he loves us tenderly."

Congress awarded him a pension of $2500 a year in 1790, lasting until his death. Baron von Steuben never married and had no children. He adopted Captain Benjamin Walker and Major General William North as his heirs. This was a common practice by gay men in an era before same-sex marriage. However, the historical record is not clear about how close these men were in their relationship and whether it was sexual. These men lived together and managed his finances. John Mulligan, also gay, served as the baron's secretary and also had a relationship with him.

Baron von Steuben died at his Oneida County estate on November 28, 1794. He was buried in a grove at what is now the Steuben Memorial State Historic Site. He left his estate to his companions, Walker and North, with whom he had "extraordinarily intense emotional relationship . . . treating them as surrogate sons." He also considered Mulligan similarly and left him his vast library, map collection, and $2500 in cash. North divided the land among his military companions. Today, the estate is part of the town of Steuben, New York.

In memory of the baron, von Steuben Day is celebrated every September in many cities in the United States, often considered the year's German American event. In New York City, the German American

Baron Friedrich Wilhelm von Steuben (1730–1794)

The tomb of General von Steuben.

Steuben Parade is held in September, after which an Oktoberfest celebration begins. Chicago's Steuben Day parade was featured in the movie *Ferris Bueller's Day Off*. Philadelphia also has a smaller parade.

The Steuben Society was founded in 1919 to help German-American communities after World War I. It is one of the largest organizations for German Americans.

Several ships have been named after the baron, the most recent being the U.S. Navy submarine USS *Von Steuben*.

Counties in New York and Indiana carry his name. The city of Steubenville, Ohio, is named after the baron. Several buildings and facilities are also named in his honor, and his former New Jersey home is a historic site.

A statue of the baron in Lafayette Square, in Washington, DC, joins statues from three other European military leaders who assisted the Revolution. There are other statues of von Steuben around the country, including at the Valley Forge Military Park.

Actors have portrayed von Steuben on television over the years. In 1979, Nehemiah Persoff played the general in the miniseries *The Rebels*. Kurt Knudson played him in the 1984 miniseries *George Washington*. Arnold Schwarzenegger provided the voice of von Steuben in the animated series *Liberty's Kids*. A documentary titled *Von Steuben's Continentals: The First American Army* was released on DVD in 2007. It detailed the improvements made by the general at Valley Forge.

Hugh Williamson
(1735 – 1819)

"The Ben Franklin of North Carolina"

Trinity Church Cemetery
New York, New York

US Constitution • First US Congress

Hugh Williamson was a Pennsylvania-born physician, scholar, and politician who was elected to the Continental Congress, where he signed the US Constitution on behalf of North Carolina. He lived in several states during his lifetime and was known as North Carolina's Benjamin Franklin.

Williamson, born December 5, 1735, in West Nottingham Township, Chester County, Pennsylvania, was the son of John Williamson, a clothier, and his wife, Mary (née Davison) Williamson. The Williamsons were devout Presbyterians of Scots-Irish descent. Apparently too frail for the family's clothier business, Williamson was encouraged to become a minister and was sent to Francis Alison's New London Academy near Newark, Delaware, graduating in 1754.

Upon graduation, Williamson spent the next three years studying mathematics at the College of Philadelphia, the predecessor of the University of Pennsylvania. He graduated in the school's first class on May 17, 1757, five days before his father died.

Over the next few years, as he settled his father's estate, he tutored Latin at the Philadelphia Academy and continued his theological studies

Hugh Williamson

with Reverend Samuel Finley, his neighbor in West Nottingham, who later became the president of the College of New Jersey. Williamson moved to Connecticut and obtained a preacher's license but was disillusioned by the divisions in the Presbyterian Church and burdened by ill health. He turned again to academics and completed a master's degree at the College of Philadelphia in 1760 and joined the faculty as a professor of mathematics.

However, Williamson continued to study and became interested in the human body and its functions. He studied medicine at the University of Edinburgh and the University of Utrecht in the Netherlands. He received his medical degree on August 6, 1764, and returned to Philadelphia to open a practice. A polymath, he also continued other scientific pursuits and projects, landing membership in the American Philosophical Society in 1768 and acclaim in Europe in intellectual circles for his work on the transits of Venus and Mercury and his papers "An Attempt to Account for the Change in Climate" and "An Essay on Comets." All contained original ideas, leading to an honorary doctorate from the University of Leyden in the Netherlands.

Hugh Williamson (1735–1819)

In 1773, to raise money for a new academy in Newark, Delaware, Williamson traveled to the West Indies and then to Europe, stopping in Boston in mid-December. There, he witnessed the Boston Tea Party on December 18, as Patriots disguised as Indians tossed crates of tea into the harbor in protest of Parliament's tax.

Upon reaching England a few weeks later, Williamson was summoned before the Privy Council to testify regarding the rebellion in Boston and colonial affairs generally. He warned the councilors that there would be further trouble if policies were not changed. At the time, he was collaborating with Benjamin Franklin in London on electrical experiments. Williamson published an anonymous "Plea of the Colonies," hoping to encourage sympathetic Whigs to side with the Americans. He also may have been involved in the controversy regarding Benjamin Franklin, the colonial postmaster, and the letters of Massachusetts Royal Governor Thomas Hutchinson which called for an abridgment of colonial rights. He stayed in England, in scientific circles, for a while before moving on to the Netherlands. He was there in July 1776 when the colonies declared independence.

Williamson returned to Philadelphia in early 1777 and volunteered as a doctor in the Continental Army. He thought his best contribution would be procuring medications, so he headed to Charleston, South Carolina, to open a business in partnership with his brother John. The goal was to obtain scarce items from the West Indies that would circumvent the British blockades.

Later, on his way to Baltimore, he was waylaid in Edenton, North Carolina, and decided to make his base of operations there. Williamson quickly became connected to the government in North Carolina, answering the call of Major General and Governor Richard Caswell to be the state's Physician and Surgeon General. Williamson accepted and held the post until the end of the Revolution.

By 1780, Williamson worked as a field surgeon, treating troops in South Carolina following the stunning defeat of American forces in Charleston. After the Battle of Camden, Williamson insisted on attending to victims on both sides of the conflict due to widespread smallpox. He then joined Major General Nathanael Greene's campaign to liberate the South.

After the war, Williamson was elected to the North Carolina House of Commons and the Continental Congress in 1782. He brought with him a Federalist perspective. In 1786, North Carolina selected Williamson to attend the Annapolis Convention but arrived too late to have an impact. The following year, he was appointed to the Constitutional Convention in Philadelphia. There, he lodged with Alexander Hamilton and James Madison and led the North Carolina delegation. Though personally opposed to slavery, Williamson voted for the "Three-Fifths Compromise" that permitted its continuance. Near the end of the convention, Williamson wrote what was known as the "Letters of Sylvius," urging North Carolina to ratify the Constitution. The decision was whether the United States would remain a "system of patchwork and a series of expedients" or become "the most flourishing, independent, and happy nation on the face of the earth." Thomas Jefferson summed up Williamson's contributions, noting he was "a very useful member, of an acute mind, attentive to business, and of a high degree of erudition."

After he signed the US Constitution, Williamson returned to the Congress in New York to wrap up. He then returned to North Carolina to urge its ratification, saying it was "more free and more perfect than any form of government that has ever been adopted by any nation."

Williamson was elected to the First Federal Congress and served two terms. He opposed the establishment of the Bank of the United States, the federal government's assumption of state debt, the whiskey excise tax, and the Jay Treaty.

Williamson finally married Maria Apthorpe, the daughter of Charles Ward Apthorpe, in January 1789. The couple had two sons, but Maria died during the birth of their second child in 1790. The child died soon after. Williamson decided not to run again for Congress and retired to New York City. There, he continued to write and research and raise his son, who perished in 1811 at the age of 22.

Over the years, Williamson published a wide range of works, including a two-volume *History of North Carolina* (1812). He advocated for inland canals, leading later to the Erie Canal. He was also a trustee or founding member of the University of North Carolina, the New York College of Physicians and Surgeons, and the New York Literary and Philosophical

Society. His philanthropy involved the support and development of an orphan asylum, the humane society, and a hospital dispensary. He was also a prominent member of the New York Historical Society, and in 1813, Williamson was elected to the American Antiquarian Society.

Williamson died suddenly in New York City on May 22, 1819, while driving his carriage. He was 83. He was buried in Trinity Churchyard in New York City, near the grave of Alexander Hamilton.

Williamson Counties in Tennessee and Illinois were named for him. Williamson Street in Madison, Wisconsin, also carries his name.

Grave of Hugh Williamson

Henry Wisner
(c 1720 – 1790)

Gunpowder Patriot

Buried at Old Wallkill Cemetery,
Phillipsburg, New York.

Continental Association • Finance

Henry Wisner was a patriot leader during the American Revolution and represented New York in the Continental Congress. If he hadn't hurried home to Goshen, New York right after the vote for independence, to make gunpowder for the coming hostilities, he likely would have signed the Declaration of Independence on August 2. His story is a bit unusual.

The precise date of his birth is unknown but was around 1720 in Florida, New York, a little village in Orange County. Wisner lived his entire life as a resident of Orange County. His family originally came to America from Switzerland in 1710. Henry married Sarah Norton from Queens County on Long Island, probably around 1740 and they settled in Goshen, New York where he built and operated a gristmill and became one of the town's leading citizens. Although he received the ordinary local education he was trusted and was appointed the justice of the peace.

In 1759, he was elected a member of the Colonial Assembly of New York and continued to serve there for eleven consecutive terms until 1769. He was a member of the first county committee to consider the difficulty between Great Britain and the American colonies. In 1768, he

Henry Wisner (c 1720 – 1790)

Monument in honor of Henry Wisner in Goshen, New York
(photo by Lawrence Knorr).

became a judge in the county's court of common pleas. His zeal led him to be named a delegate from Orange County, to the first Congress which convened at Philadelphia, in the fall of 1774. When New York created a revolutionary government in 1775, Wisner was sent to the New York Provincial Congress. That body named him a delegate to the Second Continental Congress, where he served until 1776.

New York, at this time, was clearly anxious to maintain peace and doubtful of the policy of independence. In December, the New York Convention had voted that only five of the twelve delegates that had originally been appointed, should continue at Philadelphia and that any three should be considered a quorum to represent the colony. On June 8, 1776, the delegates wrote home for instructions and were told they had no authority to vote for a break with England. On July 2, twelve of the thirteen colonies voted that the united colonies are free and independent states. Every other hesitating colony had withdrawn its instructions or left its delegates free to follow the general feeling, strongly in favor of independence. The New York delegation feeling the awkwardness of their position wrote to the Congress of New York and explained that there was not a single dissenting vote for independence. The New York delegates had not voted on July 2 and were silent again on the formal adoption of the declaration on July 4. Finally, on July 9, New York's Congress reversed its instructions and on August 2, it was signed by all the delegates then present. Wisner had left Philadelphia and was not present on that occasion. A claim made years later and stated on the monument in Goshen that Wisner was the only member of the New York delegation to vote in favor of independence seems to be without foundation. He did not vote because he could not vote.

Wisner had learned while serving in Congress that the Continental Army was desperate for powder and shot. When he returned home he built three gunpowder mills. At their height, he was shipping 1,000 pounds of gunpowder to the Army each week. He later financed the erection of cannon and other defensive works overlooking the Hudson River that blocked the British ability to use the river. Both the Americans and the British knew that passage on the Hudson was strategically important. In late 1776, Wisner along with Gilbert Livingston sounded the Hudson River, and as part of a Secret Committee of the Committee of Safety, recommended the placement of chains in strategic locations along the Hudson. The Americans eventually constructed such chains. The largest and most important was the Great Chain between West Point and Constitution Island which was reset each spring until the end of the war.

In 1777, while serving in the provincial congress, Wisner served as a member of the committee that drafted the first constitution of the state of New York. Under that constitution, he served as a state senator from 1777 until 1782. In 1788, Wisner was a delegate to the state convention

Henry Wisner (c 1720–1790)

called to ratify the U.S. Constitution. He was one of those who opposed ratification fearing too much power was granted to the central government, which would eventually infringe on individual rights.

Henry Wisner died at home in Goshen in 1790 and is buried in the Old Wallkill Cemetery in Phillipsburg, New York. At this writing, his grave is very badly weather-beaten and his name can barely be made out on the stone. There is nothing around his grave that tells anything about him. As mentioned above there is a nice monument to his memory in Goshen on which is the claim that he was the only New Yorker who voted for the Declaration of Independence.

Grave of Henry Wisner at Old Wallkill Cemetery in Phillipsburg, New York (photo by Lawrence Knorr).

Sources

Books, Magazines, Journals, Files:

Alexander, Edward P. *Revolutionary Conservative: James Duane of New York*. New York: Ams Press, 1978.

Anthony, Katharine Susan. *First Lady of the Revolution; The Life of Mercy Otis Warren*. Port Washington, N.Y.: Kennikat Press, 1972.

Appleby, Joyce. *Inheriting the Revolution: The First Generation of Americans*. Cambridge, Massachusetts: Harvard University Press, 2000.

Atkinson, Rick. *The British Are Coming: The War for America, Lexington to Princeton, 1775-1777*. New York: Henry Holt & Co. 2019.

Bordewich, Fergus M. *The First Congress: How James Madison, George Washington, and a Group of Extraordinary Men Invented the Government*. New York: Simon and Schuster Paperbacks, 2016.

Boudreau, George W. *Independence: A Guide to Historic Philadelphia*. Yardley, Pennsylvania: Westholme Publishing, LLC. 2012.

Bowen, Catherine Drinker. *Miracle at Philadelphia: The Story of the Constitutional Convention May to September 1787*. Boston, Massachusetts: Little, Brown & Company, 1966.

Breen, T.H, *George Washington's Journey: The President Forges a New Nation*. New York: Simon & Schuster. 2016.

Brookhiser, Richard. *Gentleman Revolutionary: Gouverneur Morris The Rake Who Wrote the Constitution*. New York: Free Press, 2003.

———. *John Marshall: The Man Who Made the Supreme Court*. New York: Basic Books. 2018.

Brush, Edward Hale. *Rufus King and His Times*. New York: N.L. Brown, 1926.

Chadwick, Bruce. I Am Murdered: *George Wythe, Thomas Jefferson, and the Killing That Shocked a New Nation*. Hoboken, New Jersey: John Wiley & Sons, 2009.

Chambers, II, John Whiteclay. *The Oxford Companion to American Military History*. Oxford: Oxford University Press, 1999.

Commager, Henry Steele & Richard B. Morris. *The Spirit of 'Seventy-Six: The Story of the American Revolution as Told by Participants*. New York: Harper & Rowe, 1967.

Cole, Ryan. *Light-Horse Harry Lee: The Rise and Fall of a Revolutionary Hero*. Washington, D.C.: Regnery History. 2019.

Conlin, Joseph R. *The Morrow Book of Quotations in American History*. New York: William Morrow and Company, Inc., 1984.

Daniels, Jonathan. *Ordeal of Ambition*. Garden City, New York: Doubleday & Company, Inc., 1970.

Dann, John C. *The Revolution Remembered: Eyewitness Accounts of the War for Independence*. Chicago: University of Chicago Press, 1980.

SOURCES

DeRose, Chris. *Founding Rivals: Madison vs. Monroe: The Bill of Rights and the Election that Saved a Nation*. New York: MJF Books, 2011.

Drury, Bob & Tom Clavin. *Valley Forge*. New York: Simon & Schuster. 2018.

Ellis, Joseph J. *Revolutionary Summer: The Birth of American Independence*. New York: Alfred A. Knopf, 2013.

———. *The Quartet: Orchestrating the Second American Revolution, 1783-1789*. New York: Alfred A. Knopf, 2015.

———. *His Excellency: George Washington*. New York: Alfred A. Knopf, 2004.

Flexner, James Thomas. *George Washington in the American Revolution, 1775-1783*. Boston: Little, Brown & Company, 1967.

Flower, Lenore Embick. "Visit of President George Washington to Carlisle, 1794." Carlisle, Pennsylvania: The Hamilton Library and Cumberland County Historical Society, 1932.

Gerlach, Don R. *Proud Patriot: Philip Schuyler and the War of Independence, 1775-1783*. Syracuse, N.Y.: Syracuse University Press, 1987.

Goodrich, Charles A. *Lives of the Signers of the Declaration of Independence*. Charlotteville, N.Y.: SamHar Press, 1976.

Griffith, IV, William R. *The Battle of Lake George: England's First Triumph in the French and Indian War*. Charleston, South Carolina: The History Press, 2016.

Grossman, Mark. *Encyclopedia of the Continental Congress*. Armenia, New York: Grey House Publishing, 2015.

Hamilton, Edward P. *Fort Ticonderoga: Key to a Continent*. Boston: Little, Brown & Company, 1964.

Isenberg, Nancy. *Fallen Founder: The Life of Aaron Burr*. New York: Penguin Group, 2007.

Kennedy, Roger G. *Burr, Hamilton, and Jefferson: A Study in Character*. New York: Oxford University Press, 1999.

Kiernan, Denise & Joseph D'Agnese. *Signing Their Lives Away: The Fame and Misfortune of the Men Who Signed the Declaration of Independence*. Philadelphia: Quirk Books, 2008.

———. *Signing Their Rights Away: The Fame and Misfortune of the Men Who Signed the United States Constitution*. Philadelphia: Quirk Books, 2011.

Klarman, Michael J. *The Framers' Coup: The Making of the United States Constitution*. New York: Oxford University Press, 2016.

Langguth, A. J. *Patriots*. New York: Simon and Schuster, 1988.

Larson, Edward J. *A Magnificient Catastrophe*. New York: Free Press, 2007.

Lee, Mike. Written *Out of History: The Forgotten Founders Who Fought Big Government*. New York: Penguin Books, 2017.

Lewis, James E., Jr., *The Burr Conspiracy: Uncovering the Story of an Early American Crisis*, Princeton: Princeton University Press, 2017.

Lockridge, Ross Franklin. *The Harrisons*. 1941.

Lomask, Milton. *Aaron Burr: The Years from Princeton to Vice President, 1756-1805*. New York: Farrar Straus Giroux, 1979.

Lossing, Benson J. *Pictorial Field Book of the Revolution*. New York: Harper Brothers. 1851.

Maier, Pauline. *American Scripture: Making the Declaration of Independence*. New York: Alfred A. Knopf, Inc., 1997.

McCullough, David. *John Adams*. New York: Simon & Schuster, 2002.

Meltzer, Brad & Josh Mensch. *The First Conspiracy: The Secret Plot to Kill George Washington*. New York: Flat Iron Books. 2018.

Middlekauff, Robert. *The Glorious Cause: The American Revolution, 1763-1789*. Oxford: Oxford University Press, 2005.

Miller, Jr., Arthur P. & Marjorie L. Miller. *Pennsylvania Battlefields and Military Landmarks*. Mechanicsburg, Pennsylvania: Stackpole Books, 2000.

Millett, Allan R. & Peter Maslowski. *For the Common Defense: A Military History of the United States of America*. New York: The Free Press, 1984.

Moore, Charles. *The Family Life of George Washington*. New York: Houghton Mifflin, 1926.

Nagel, Paul C. *The Lees of Virginia: Seven Generations of an American Family*. Oxford: Oxford University Press, 1990.

O'Connell, Robert L. *Revolutionary: George Washington at War*. New York: Random House. 2019.

Racove, Jack N. *Revolutionaries: A New History of the Invention of America*. New York: Houghton Mifflin Harcourt, 2011.

Raphael, Ray. Founding Myths: *Stories That Hide Our Patriotic Past*. New York: MJF Books, 2004.

Rossiter, Clinton. *1787 The Grand Convention*. New York: The Macmillan Company, 1966.

Seymour, Joseph. *The Pennsylvania Associators, 1747-1777*. Yardley, Pennsylvania: Westholme Publishing, LLC. 2012.

Schweikart, Larry & Michael Allen. *A Patriot's History of the United States from Columbus's Great Discovery to the War on Terror*. New York: Penguin, 2004.

Sharp, Arthur G. *Not Your Father's Founders*. Avon, Massachusetts: Adams Media, 2012.

Stahr, Walter. *John Jay: Founding Father*. New York: Diversion Books, 2017.

Taafee, Stephen R. *The Philadelphia Campaign, 1777-1778*. Lawrence, Kansas: University of Kansas Press, 2003.

Tinkcom, Harry Marlin, *The Republicans and the Federalists in Pennsylvania, 1790-1801*. Harrisburg, Pennsylvania: Pennsylvania Historical and Museum Commission. 1950.

Ward, Matthew C. *Breaking the Backcountry: The Seven Years' War in Virginia and Pennsylvania, 1754-1765*. Pittsburgh, Pennsylvania: University of Pittsburgh Press, 2003.

Weisberger, Bernard A. *America Afire: Jefferson, Adams, and the Revolutionary Election of 1800*. New York: HarperCollins, 2000.

Wood, Gordon S. *The Radicalism of the American Revolution*. New York: Vintage Books, 1993.

———. *Empire of Liberty: A History of the Early Republic, 1789-1815*. New York: Penguin Books, 2004.

———. *Revolutionary Characters: What Made the Founders Different*. New York: Penguin Books, 2006.

SOURCES

———. *The Americanization of Benjamin Franklin*. Oxford: Oxford University Press, 2009.

Wright, Benjamin F. *The Federalist: The Famous Papers on the Principles of American Government: Alexander Hamilton, James Madison, John Jay*. New York: Metro Books, 2002.

Zobel, Hiller B. *The Boston Massacre*. New York: W. W. Norton & Company, 1970.

Video Resources:

Guelzo, Allen C. The Great Courses: *America's Founding Fathers* (Course N. 8525). Chantilly, Virginia: The Teaching Company, 2017.

Online Resources:

Archives.gov – for information on the Constitutional Convention.
CauseofLiberty.blogspot.com – for information on Daniel Carroll.
ColonialHall.com – for information about the signers of the Declaration of Independence.
DSDI1776.com – for information on many Founders.
FamousAmericans.net – for information on many Founders.
FindaGrave.com – for burial information, vital statistics and obituaries.
FirstLadies.org – for information on Abigail Adams.
Newspapers.com – Hundreds of newspaper articles were accessed—too numerous to mention here.
NPS.gov – for information on various park sites.
TeachingAmericanHistory.com – for information on Charles Pinckney and George Wythe.
TheHistoryJunkie.com – for information on multiple Founders.
USHistory.org – for information on multiple Founders.
Wikipedia.com – for general historical information.

Index

Adams, John, 7–8, 24, 29, 36, 42, 47, 65–67, 71, 85, 104, 110, 120
Adams, John Quincy, 9, 77
Aitken, Robert, 109
Albany, NY, 5, 8, 47, 49, 51, 87, 89–90, 101, 115, 120–23, 125
Albany Rural Cemetery, Menands, NY, 115, 120-21, 125
Alexander, Catherine, 29
Alexander, James, 90–91
Alexander, Mary Spratt Provoost, 90
Alexander, William (Lord Stirling), 29, 41, 90–91
Alison, Francis, 135
Alsop, Abigail (née Sackett), 13
Alsop, John, 5, 13–17, 75, 81
Alsop, John Sr., 13
Alsop, Joseph, 16
Alsop, Lucy, 16
Alsop, Mary, 14–15, 75
Alsop, Richard (ancestor), 13
Alsop, Richard (brother), 14
Alsop, Richard (nephew), 16
Alsop, Richard (grandnephew), 16
American Academy of the Arts and Sciences, 92
American Antiquarian Society, 139
American Philosophical Society, 91, 112, 120, 136
André, John, 131
Annapolis Convention, 138
Annesley, Edward, 78–79
Annesley, Elizabeth, 79, 81
Antifederalist, 3, 7–8, 86
Antill, Mary, 106
Apthorpe, Charles Ward, 138
Apthorpe, Maria, 138
Armstrong, John Jr., 42
Arnold, Benedict, 40–41, 123
Articles of Confederation, 21, 24, 27, 29, 45, 62, 68, 75, 78, 81, 86, 95

Bache, Richard, 109
Baltimore, MD, 40, 137
Bank of New York, 30
Bank of North America, 111
Bank of the United States, 10, 30, 51, 138
Barber, Francis, 91
Barclay, Henry, 2, 89
Barren Hill, Battle of, 131
Basking Ridge, NJ, 29

Beekman, Stephen D., 5
Bell, Cornelia, 117
Benson, Eva, 21
Berkeley Heights, NJ, 94
Berlin, Irving, 17
Bill of Rights, 3
Boerum, Jacob Willemse Van, 18
Boerum, John, 19
Boerum Park, 20
Boerum, Rachel (née Bloom), 18
Boerum, Simon, 5, 18–20
Boerum, William 18
Bonaparte, Napolean, 113
Boston, MA, 23, 40, 53–58, 60–61, 64–65, 80, 129, 137
Boston, Massacre, 53, 55
Boston Tea Party, 53, 60, 64, 137
Boudinot, Elias, 92
Bowen, Catherine Drinker, 97
Bowers-Livingston-Osborn House, 92
Brace, C. Loring IV, 16
Brace, Charles Loring, 17
Brace, Gerald Warner, 16
Brack, Danae, 109
Braddock Expedition, 37–39
Bradstreet, John, 123
Bragdon, Isabella, 73
Brearly, David, 93, 117
Bronx, NY, 1, 83, 95, 99, 101–102, 105, 125
Brookhaven, NY, 32, 36
Brooklyn, NY, 18–20, 89, 93
Brooklyn, Battle of (also Brooklyn Heights), 81
Brunswick, NJ, 110
Brush, Edward Hale, 74
Bunner, Anna Bedford, 29
Bunner, Rudolph, 29
Burgoyne, John, 40, 86, 125
Burr, Aaron, 1, 3, 8, 35, 46–47, 51, 70, 120, 124

Caldwell, James, 55
Calhoun, John C., 9
Camden, Battle of, 137
Camden, SC, 41
Carpender, Sarah, 103
Carroll, Charles, 36
Caswell, Richard, 137
Chalmers, James, 110
Chaney, Lon, 99

INDEX

Charleston, SC, 41, 137
Chauncey, Henry, 16
Chew, Beverly, 30
Christ Church, Duanesburg, NY, 24
Christ Episcopal Church, Duanesburg, NY, 21
Church, John, 51, 125
Clarkson, William, 33
Clay, Henry, 77
Clinton, Catherine, 5
Clinton, Charles, 3
Clinton, Cornelia Tappen, 5
Clinton, DeWitt, 8, 10
Clinton, Elizabeth (née Denniston), 3
Clinton, Elizabeth (daughter), 5
Clinton, George, 1, 3–12, 19, 34, 45, 68, 70, 76
Clinton, George Washington, 5, 34
Clinton, James, 3–5, 10
Clinton, Maria, 5
Clinton, Martha Washington, 5
Cliosophic Society, 120
Clive, Robert, 27
Cochran, John, 125
Colfax, William, 125
Columbia University (also King's College), 17, 29, 44, 63, 84, 91, 95
Committee of Fifty, 80
Committee of Five, 2, 84–85, 110
Committee of Sixty, 15, 23, 80
Congressional Cemetery, Washington, DC, 10
Constitution (New Jersey), 116
Constitution (New York), 5, 24, 29, 34, 68, 86, 142
Constitution (U.S.), 1, 7, 15, 27, 30, 43, 45, 48, 62, 68–69, 73, 75, 89, 93, 95, 97–98, 104, 115, 117–18, 121, 124, 135, 138, 142–43
Continental Association, 13, 15, 18–19, 21, 23, 32, 34, 62, 65, 89, 92, 140
Conway, Thomas, 41
Conway Cabal, 41, 81, 97
Cooper, Charles, 47
Corbett, William, 114
Cornwallis, Charles, 37, 41
Cornwallis, Edward, 37
Cox, Mary, 103
Crane, Stephen (patriot), 92
Crosby, David, 17
Crosby, Floyd, 17

Dayton, Jonathan, 93, 117
Deane, Silas, 15, 111
Declaration of Independence, 2, 5, 12–13, 15, 18, 24, 32, 34, 66, 78, 81–82, 84–85, 89, 92, 98, 101, 104, 107, 110, 140, 143
De Hart, John, 92
Delafield, Julia, 80
De Lancey, James, 23, 91, 103, 122

Denning, Hannah Maria, 29
Denning, William, 29
Duane, Abraham, 21
Duer, Alexander, 30
Duane, Anthony, 21
Duane, Cornelius, 21
Duane, James, 5, 14, 21–26
Duane, John, 26
Duanesburg, NY, 21, 24–25
Duer, Catherine Alexander, 30
Duer, Denning, 31
Duer, Frances (née Frye), 27
Duer, Frances (daughter), 29
Duer, Henrietta Elizabeth, 30
Duer, James Gore King, 31
Duer, John (father), 27
Duer, John (son), 29
Duer, Maria Theodora, 30
Duer, Sarah Henrietta, 29
Duer, William (patriot), 27–31
Duer, William (congressman), 31
Duer, William Alexander, 29
Dummer Academy, 74
Duponceau, Pierre Etienne, 129, 131

Edenton, NC, 137
Elizabethtown, NJ, 91–93
Elliott, Ann B., 103
Ellis, Joseph, 67, 72
Ellsworth, Oliver, 120
Elmer, Jonathan, 118
Erie Canal Commission, 88, 98

Federalist Papers, 43, 46–47, 51, 62, 68
Federalist Party, 8, 27, 47, 69–71, 73, 76, 98, 121, 138
Finley, Samuel, 136
First Baptist Church, Boston, MA, 54
Fish, Hamilton, 94
Florida, NY, 140
Floyd, Anna, 5, 34
Floyd, Catherine, 33
Floyd, Charity, 32
Floyd, Charles, 32
Floyd, Elizabeth, 35
Floyd, Mary, 33
Floyd, Nicholl, 32
Floyd, Nicholl (son), 33
Floyd, Richard, 32
Floyd, Ruth, 32
Floyd, Tabitha (née Smith), 32
Floyd, William, 1, 5, 32–36
Flushing, NY, 79–80
Fort Clinton, 6
Fort Duquesne, 38

149

Fort Frontenac, 4, 123
Fort Lee, 110
Fort Miller, 28
Fort Montgomery, 6
Fort Oswego, 80
Fort Schuyler, 125
Fort Ticonderoga, 40, 123
Franklin, Benjamin, 15, 67, 85, 109–10, 129, 135, 137
Frederick the Great, 128–30
French, Philip, 90
French Revolution, 93, 98, 107, 112
French, Susannah, 90, 93
French, Susanna (née Brockholst), 90
Frogat, Mary, 14
Frye, Frederick, 27

Gallatin, Albert, 9
Galloway Plan, 19, 29
Garrick, Edward, 54
Gates, Dorothea, 37
Gates, Elizabeth, 37, 42
Gates, Horatio, 1, 37–42, 123
Gates, Robert (father), 37
Gates, Robert (son), 39
Gelston, David, 33
Gelston, Phoebe, 33
Genêt, Edmond-Charles, 5
Gibbs, Wolcott, 17
Glover, John, 74
Goldfinch, John, 54
Goshen, NY, 140–43
Gouverneur, Sarah, 101
Grace Episcopal Churchyard, Queens, NY, 27, 31, 77
Gracie, Archibald III, 17
Gracie, Archibald IV, 17
Grand Army of the Republic Cemetery, Richfield Springs, NY, 53, 61
Greene, Nathanael, 41, 110, 130–31
Green-Wood Cemetery, 18, 20, 89, 93–94

Hamilton, Alexander, 43–51, 68–69, 75–76, 86, 91, 95, 120–21, 124–25, 130, 138–39
Hamilton, Elizabeth Schuyler, 1, 45, 49–54, 121, 125
Hancock, John, 55
Harrison, William Henry, 93
Hartley, David, 67
Harvard University, 74
Hawkes, James, 60
Hewes, George (father), 53
Hewes, George Robert Twelves, 1, 53–61
Hewes, Robert (uncle), 53
Holker, John, 29

Hooker, Isabella Beecher, 17
Huger, Daniel, 103
Hutchinson, Thomas, 137

Iroquois, 7, 89

Jackson, Andrew, 9
Jagvodin, Elizabeth von, 127
Jamaica, NY, 1, 73
Jan, Anneke, 23
Jay, John, 1, 3, 5–6, 14–15, 24, 35, 46, 62–72, 76, 84–86, 94–95, 138
Jay, Peter, 62
Jefferson, Martha, 98
Jefferson, Thomas, 3, 7–9, 35–36, 46, 51, 70, 76, 84–86, 98, 110, 113, 138
John Jay Cemetery, Rye, NY, 62, 72
Johnson, Thomas, 119
Jones, Hannah, 33–34
Jones, William, 33

Kean, Julia, 94
Kean, Thomas, 94
Kearneysville, WV, 42
Ketaltas, Althea, 21–22
Kilroy, Matthew, 55
King, Charles, 17
King, Frederika Gore, 17
King, James G., 17
King, John Alsop, 17
King Manor, 77
King, Richard, 73
King, Rufus, 1, 8, 13, 15–16, 73–77, 124
King, Rufus (newspaper editor), 17
King, Rufus Jr. (officer), 17
King's Arms tavern, 91
Kings County, NY, 18–19
Kingston, NY, 3, 6, 10
Kirschke, James J., 104

Lafayette Square, 133
Lake George, 123
Lambert, Mary, 108
Lansing, Gerrit G., 106
Lansing, John, 106
Lansing, Sarah, 106
Laurens, Henry, 67, 111–12
Laurens, John, 111
Lawrence, Mary, 101
Lawrence, Thomas, 103
Ledyard, Henry Brockholst, 94
Lee, Arthur, 15
Lennington, Mary, 94
Lewis, Ann, 79, 82
Lewis, Amy (née Pettingal), 78

INDEX

Lewis, Francis (father), 78
Lewis, Francis, 78–83
Lewis, Francis Jr. (son), 79–80, 82
Lewis, Gabriel Ludlow, 82
Lewis, Margaret, 82
Lewis, Morgan, 79, 82
Lexington and Concord, Battles of, 5, 26
L'Hommedieu, Ezra, 32
Liberty Hall, 92
Lincoln, Benjamin, 40–41
Linn, James, 94
Little Britain, NY, 3–4
Livingston, Catherine (née Van Brugh), 90
Livingston Catherine, 93
Livingston County, KY, 88
Livingston County, NY, 88
Livingston, Edward, 106
Livingston, Edwin Brockholst, 94
Livingston, Gertrude, 79
Livingston, Gilbert, 142
Livingston, Henry Brockholst, 94
Livingston, John, 93
Livingston, John Lawrence, 94
Livingston, Judith, 94
Livingston, Manny, 82
Livingston, Margaret Beekman, 84
Livingston, Mary, 22, 94
Livingston, Maturin, 82
Livingston, New Jersey, 94
Livingston, Peter Van Brugh, 89
Livingston, Philip (father), 5, 14, 22, 80, 89, 103, 106
Livingston, Philip, 89
Livingston, Philip French, 94
Livingston, Robert, 1, 5, 22, 63–64, 80, 84–89, 91, 110
Livingston, Robert (judge), 79, 84
Livingston, Sarah, 29, 64, 66, 72, 94
Livingston, Susannah, 93
Livingston, William, 1, 64, 85, 89–94, 117–18
Livingston, William Jr., 94
Long Island, 15, 18, 32–34, 36, 104, 140
Louisiana Purchase, 84, 86
Low, Isaac, 14
Ludlow, Elizabeth, 79
Ludlow, Gabriel, 79
Lynn, MA, 59

Mackay, Ellin Travers, 17
Madison, James, 3, 8–11, 45–46, 68–70, 76, 98, 138
Malcolm, John, 58
Marshall, John, 69, 72
Mathews, David, 92
Maxwell, Thompson, 55

McHenry, James, 51
Mercer, James, 80
Middlekauff, Robert, 110
Middletown, CT, 14–15, 34
Miller, Alice Duer, 17, 31
Minor, Halsey, 17
Missouri Compromise, 77
Monckton, Robert, 39
Monmouth, Battle of, 131
Monroe, James, 47, 76, 113
Montcalm, Louis-Joseph de, 80
Montgomery, Janet, 42
Montgomery, Richard, 42, 123
Morgan, Daniel, 41
Morris, Catherine (sister), 101
Morris, Catherine (daughter), 103
Morris, Charles Manigault, 105
Morris, Daniel François van Braam, 106
Morris, Francis, 5
Morris, Gouverneur, 1, 64, 86, 95–101, 104–105
Morris, Gouverneur Jr., 98
Morris, Gouverneur (great-grandson), 99
Morris, Helena Magdalena, 103, 105
Morris, Isabella, 101
Morris, Jacob, 103
Morris, James, 103
Morris, Katrintje (née Staats), 101
Morris, Lewis I, 106
Morris, Lewis II, 101
Morris, Lewis III, 5, 98, 101–106
Morris, Lewis (grandson), 105
Morris, Lewis V., 103, 105
Morris, Mary, 103
Morris, Richard (ancestor), 102
Morris, Richard (brother), 101, 103
Morris, Richard Valentine, 103
Morris, Robert, 29–30, 50, 97, 111
Morris, Robert Hunter, 101
Morris, Sabina Elliott, 105
Morris, Sarah, 103
Morris, Staats Long, 101, 103–104, 106
Morris, William Walton, 98, 103
Morrisania, 95, 102–105
Morristown, NJ, 49–51, 102, 114
Mount Vernon, 37, 40
Muhlenberg, Frederick, 47
Mulligan, John, 132
Mutual Life Insurance Company of New York, 30

Nassau Hall, 115
Nelson, William, 31
New Bromley, NJ, 116
New Brunswick, NJ, 120
New Jersey Plan, 115, 117–18
New London Academy, 135

NEW YORK PATRIOTS

New Rochelle, NY, 1, 107, 112–14, 122
New Windsor, NY, 4, 13, 50
New York City, 4–5, 7–8, 13–16, 19, 21, 24, 27, 30, 40, 42, 44, 48, 50–52, 62–64, 69, 75, 78, 80, 82, 84–88, 90–95, 120, 132, 138–39
New York College of Physicians and Surgeons, 138
New York Historical Society, 139
New York Hospital Association, 14–15
New York Literary and Philosophical Society, 138–39
New York Manumission Society, 24, 70
Newark, DE, 135, 137
Newburgh, NY, 42, 131
Newburyport, MA, 75
Newhall's Tavern, 59
Newtown, NY, 15–16
North, William, 132
Norton, Sarah, 140

Old Dutch Churchyard, Kingston, NY, 3, 10
Old Episcopal Churchyard, Jamaica, NY, 73
Old First Reformed Church Cemetery, Brooklyn, NY, 19–20
Old Wallkill Cemetery, Phillipsburg, NY, 140, 143
Olive Branch Petition, 81
Ollive, Esther, 108
Ollive, Elizabeth, 109
Ollive, Samuel, 108
Oswald, Richard, 67
Otsego County, NY, 60

Pacific Mail Steamship Company, 16
Pain, Frances (née Cocke), 107
Pain, Joseph, 107
Paine, Thomas, 107–14
Panic of 1792, 27, 30
Parsippany, NJ, 92
Parsons, Theophilus, 74–75
Paterson, Cornelia Bell, 117
Paterson, Frances, 117
Paterson, Mary, 115
Paterson, NJ, 120
Paterson, Richard, 115
Paterson, Thomas Johnson, 119
Paterson, William, 93, 101, 115–20
Paterson, William Bell, 117
Pennsylvania, University of (also College of Philadelphia), 135–36
Persoff, Nehemiah, 134
Philadelphia, 3, 5, 14–15, 19–20, 23–24, 34, 45, 51, 64, 66, 68, 75, 79, 81, 97, 104, 109–10, 115, 117, 133, 136–38, 141–42
Philadelphia Academy, 135
Phillipsburg, NY, 140, 143
Pickering, Timothy, 120

Pinckney, Charles Cotesworth, 8, 76, 104
Pitt, Leonard, 56
Platt, James, 35
Platt, Zephaniah, 35
Pontiere, Louis de, 129
Poor, Enoch, 40
Poughkeepsie, NY, 68
Pierce, William, 75, 117
Princeton, Battle of, 40
Princeton, New Jersey, 115
Princeton University, 29, 115–16, 120
Providence, RI, 60

Quebec, Battle of (Revolution), 40–41, 125
Queens, NY, 1, 27, 31, 77, 80, 83, 140
Quincy, MA, 66

Randolph, Ann Cary, 98
Randolph, Edmund, 118, 120
Randolph, Thomas Mann, 98
Revere, Paul, 53, 65
Reynolds, James, 47, 51
Reynolds, Maria Lewis, 47, 51
Rhode Island, Battle of, 60, 74
Richardson, Ebenezer, 54–55
Richfield Springs, NY, 53, 60–61
Ridley, Matthew, 93
Roberdeau, Daniel, 110
Robertson, George, 79
Robertson, Marianne, 82
Robinson, Beverley, 29–30
Robinson, Morris, 30
Rome, NY, 132
Roosevelt, Theodore, 16
Rossiter, Clinton, 75
Rush, Benjamin, 81, 109
Rutgers University, 94
Rutherfurd, John, 103
Rutherfurd, Lewis Morris, 105
Rutherfurd, Robert Walter, 105
Rye, NY, 62–63, 72

St. Ann's Episcopal Churchyard, Bronx, NY, 95, 98, 101, 105
St. Clair, Arthur, 40, 123–24
St. Paul's Church, Tivoli, NY, 84, 88
St. Thomas Church, Floral Park, NY, 31
Saratoga, Battle of, 37, 40, 123
Saratoga, NY, 28, 123–24
Scarborough, MA, 73
Schenectady, NY, 23
Schenk, Maria, 18–19
Schuyler, Angelica, 50–51, 125
Schuyler, Catherine, 124
Schuyler, Cornelia (née Van Cortlandt), 121

INDEX

Schuyler, Hester, 125
Schuyler, Johannes Jr., 121
Schuyler, Johannes Sr., 121
Schuyler, John, 125
Schuyler, Margaret, 125
Schuyler, Peter, 125
Schuyler, Philip (son), 125
Schuyler, Philip John, 5–6, 28, 30, 40, 45, 49–50, 101, 121–26
Schwarzenegger, Arnold, 134
Scott, George Lewis, 109
Scott, John Morin, 6, 91
Seider, Christopher, 54
Sharp, Arthur G., 67
Shepherdstown, WV, 40
Sherburne, Henry, 74–75
Sherman, Roger, 85, 110
Smedley, Samuel, 60
Smith, John Witherspoon, 29
Smith, Samuel Stanhope, 29
Smith, Tangier, 32
Smith, William Jr., 4, 90–92
Smith, William Sr., 90, 95–96
Society of the Cincinnati, 7, 35, 42, 104, 124, 132
Southampton, NY, 33
Stahr, Walter, 64–65
Stamp Act, 73, 80
Steuben, Baron Frederick von, 127–34
Steuben, NY, 127, 132
Steuben State Memorial Site, Steuben, NY, 127, 133
Steuben, Wilhelm von, 127
Stevens, John, 85
Stevens, Mary, 85
Stockton, Richard, 82, 116
Strong, Banajah, 34
Strong, Joanna, 34
Strong, Martha (née Mills), 34
Strouppe, Peter, 122
Sullivan, John, 40
Sumner, Charles Richard, 82
Sumner, John Bird, 82
Sumner, Sarah "Sally," 54
Symmes, John Cleves, 93

Tallmadge, Benjamin, 33
Tallmadge, Matthias B., 5
Tappen, Peter, 5
Tappen, Sarah, 5
Taylor, Alan Shaw, 11
Taylor, John, 5
Ten Broeck, Abraham, 125
Ten Broeck, Elizabeth, 125
Thatcher, Benjamin Bussey, 61
Thomas, Margaret, 32
Thomson, Charles, 65

Three-Fifths Compromise, 138
Tivoli, NY, 84, 88
Treaty of Paris, 62, 70, 94
Trenton, Battle of, 40
Trenton, NJ, 67
Trinity Churchyard, Manhattan, 13, 15–16, 23, 37, 42–43, 48–49, 52, 78, 82, 93, 135, 139
Trumbull, Jonathan, 12, 34, 44, 125

Ulster County, NY, 3–4, 6

Valcour Island, Battle of, 40
Valens, Mary, 42
Valley Forge, 7, 81, 97, 129, 131, 133–34
Van Braam Houckgeest, Andreas, 103
Van Braam Houckgeest, Everarda, 103
Van Brugh, Pieter, 89
Van Buren, Martin, 35
Van Cortland, Augustus, 103
Van Cortland, Frederick, 103
Van Cortland, Helen, 103
Van Cortland, Mary, 63
Van Cortlandt, Pierre Jr., 5
Van Reeds van Oudtshoorn, Catharina C.G., 103
Van Rensselaer, Catherine, 49, 122
Van Rensselaer, Cornelia Paterson, 120
Van Rensselaer, Elizabeth, 125
Van Rensselaer, Philip Schuyler, 101
Van Rensselaer, Stephen, 35, 101, 120, 125
Vermont, 7, 30

Waddington, Mary Alsop King, 17
Walker, Benjamin, 131–32
Walton, Anne, 103
Walton, Mary, 102
Warren, Joseph, 58
Washington, DC, 10, 30, 82–83, 104, 133
Washington, George, 2–3, 5–8, 15, 24, 26, 33, 35, 37, 39–46, 49–52, 59, 62, 66–67, 69–70, 76, 81, 84, 86, 97, 104, 111, 113, 119, 123, 125, 127, 129–31, 134
Washington, Martha, 59
Watkins, John W., 94
Wayne, Anthony, 103
Wellman, William A., 82
West Nottingham Township, Chester County, PA, 135–36
West Point, 17, 98, 142
Westcott, Ann Maria, 30
Westcott, David M., 30
Westernville, NY, 35–36
Westernville Cemetery, Oneida County, NY, 32, 35–36
Westchester County, NY, 72, 104
Whiskey Rebellion, 120

White, Anthony Walton, 101
White, Euphemia, 117
White Plains, NY, 103
Wild, Philip, 100
Wilkinson, James, 41
Williamson, Hugh, 135–39
Williamson, John, 135, 137
Williamson, Mary (née Davison), 135
Wisner, Henry, 140–43
Wisner, William, 5

Witherspoon, John, 29, 82
Woodhull, Nathaniel, 32
Wrentham, MA, 58, 60
Wyatt, Jane, 17

Yale University, 16, 89, 102
Yates, Robert, 35
York, Pennsylvania, 42, 81, 129
Yorktown, Battle of, 43, 45, 51, 124, 131
Young, Alfred, 61

www.ingramcontent.com/pod-product-compliance
Lightning Source LLC
Chambersburg PA
CBHW010855090426
42737CB00019B/3382